Lois Gray

Panic
Attacks
WORKBOOK

D0791599

"Dr. Carbonell has written a wonderful, inspiring and comprehensive guidebook for winning over panic attacks. While panic attacks are terrifying for the sufferer, they take over territory in a person's life by playing a very simple but powerful game. In *Panic Attacks Workbook* you will find the solid and clever strategies needed to win this mental game and take back your life."

—R. Reid Wilson, Ph.D.
author of *Don't Panic: Taking Control of Anxiety Attacks*

Panic Attacks
WORKBOOK

**A Guided Program
for Beating the Panic Trick**

David Carbonell, Ph.D.

Ulysses Press

For my Mom, Ellen, and Adam

Text Copyright © 2004 David Carbonell. Graphics Copyright © 2004 Ulysses Press and its licensors. All rights reserved under International and Pan-American Copyright Conventions, including the right to reproduce this book or portions thereof in any form whatsoever, except for use by a reviewer in connection with a review.

Published by: Ulysses Press
                P.O. Box 3440
                Berkeley, CA 94703
                www.ulyssespress.com

The diagnostic criteria on pages 15–18 is reprinted with permission from the Diagnostic and Statistical Manual of Mental Disorders, Copyright 2000. American Psychiatric Association.

The AWARE five-step process material is used with permission from *Anxiety Disorders and Phobias: A Cognitive Perspective* by Aaron Beck, Gary Emery, and Ruth Greenberg. New York: Basic Books, Inc., 1985.

Library of Congress Control Number: 2004101024
ISBN10: 1-56975-415-2
ISBN13: 978-1-56975-415-3

Printed in Canada by Transcontinental Printing

10 9 8 7 6

Editor: Richard Harris
Editorial and production staff: Ashley Chase, Claire Chun, Lily Chou, Leslie Henriques,
   Lisa Kester, James Meetze, Lee Micheaux
Design: Sarah Levin

Distributed by Publishers Group West

The author has made every effort to trace copyright owners. Where the author has failed, he offers his apologies and undertakes to make proper acknowledgment where possible in reprints.

This book has been written and published strictly for informational purposes, and in no way should it be used as a substitute for consultation with a health-care professional. You should not consider educational material herein to be the practice of medicine or to replace consultation with a physician or other medical practitioner. The author and publisher are providing you with information in this work so that you can have the knowledge and can choose, at your own risk, to act on that knowledge. The author and publisher also urge all readers to be aware of their health status and to consult health professionals before beginning any health program, including changes in dietary habits.

Table of Contents

....

Introduction

This is a workbook for people with panic attacks and phobias. There's good news and bad news about panic attacks, and the phobias that usually accompany them.

Let's take the bad news first. The bad news is that panic is a devious, insidious trick that can make you a prisoner in your own life, home and head. It can intimidate you into abandoning the activities and situations that used to be a part of your life, like driving, air travel, public speaking, shopping in large stores, socializing, traveling freely away from your home, and many other ordinary activities. And it does this to millions of people around the world.

Even as it does this to millions of people, it also leaves them with the impression that they're "the only one" to have this strange problem. Nothing could be further from the truth. But when people think that panic is some uniquely personal problem that they have created, rather than a disorder that affects millions of people around the globe, they tend to feel ashamed and embarrassed, and retreat into a shell of shame and secrecy.

The good news is that it's only a trick. It's a very effective trick, certainly, and takes a lot of work to overcome. But it's just a trick. People can, and do, overcome this trick, and I'm going to show you how you can.

Why do I call it a trick? Not just because it fools you into thinking that you're in immediate danger of a personal catastrophe, like death, insanity, or terrible humiliation. Not only because it intimidates you into giving up so many ordinary activities you used to enjoy and take for granted. Those are terrible tricks that can rob your life of joy and meaning. But bad as they are, they're not the worst part of panic. The worst part of the panic trick is that it brainwashes you into acting and thinking in precisely the ways that make the problem worse rather than better. It tricks you into using all your personal strengths and intelligence in ways that produce a more chronic and difficult problem, rather than the recovery you seek. It uses your desire to feel "safe" to trick you into staying stuck.

I'm going to show you what to do about it. This book will expose the trick and take you, step by step, through the process of recovery.

When people first experience panic attacks, they don't really know what they're up against, and they have a hard time finding out. They don't know if they have a disease, a damaged heart, a breathing problem, a "chemical imbalance," an emotional problem, a mental problem, or what. They may go from doctor to doctor, test to test, trying to find an answer.

Along the way, they become fearful and confused. It often seems that the harder they try to put it behind them, the more it persists. They eventually come to believe one, or both, of two misleading explanations for their failure to get better.

Either they think they're too weak, or troubled, or defective in some way to recover; or they think the problem is so difficult that recovery is impossible. Both of these beliefs are untrue. This is a very treatable problem, and people can get over it. So why do so many people have so much trouble solving it?

The answer is that they don't find out that panic attacks literally "trick" them into thinking, and acting, in precisely the ways that strengthen and maintain the panic. They keep falling for the trick. Even when they recognize they're being fooled somehow, they keep falling for it.

Sometimes, when you've been fooled for a long time, you start to feel so pessimistic and bitter that you no longer hold out hope for a recovery. That's a tragedy, because this is a very treatable problem.

I'm a psychologist who specializes in helping people with anxiety. This book incorporates most of what I've learned in nearly 20 years of helping people overcome panic and phobias. I've had a lot of training in those years, and I've learned a lot from my own fear of heights, but the most valuable lessons about how to help people recover from panic have come from my clients. This opportunity to create a workbook brings the process full circle, and I'm grateful for the opportunity to pass on what I've learned.

I remember distinctly how my education about panic began. In 1984, I was interning in the mental health clinic at Hines Veterans Hospital near Chicago. I was a very green intern, conducting an intake session with a man who became increasingly annoyed with me as I clumsily tried to collect all the information the federal government, and my supervisor, required. Because he was so irritable I asked him if I had offended him somehow. He told me that he was a long-term patient at the clinic who, because he had missed two appointments with his psychiatrist, was demoted to the status of new patient, and had to go through the intake process all over again. His punishment for missing two appointments was having to talk to me, and he asked if I would please get it over with so he could get his medication.

I finally got to the part of the interview when I asked him to describe his problem. He said "panic attacks." Since the form contained several lines for me to record his answer, I dutifully asked him to tell me more. To which he replied "Panic attacks! You know what a panic attack is, don't you?"

Unfortunately for me, I didn't.

I must have overslept the day it was discussed in graduate school. I could tell it had something to do with fear, but that was the extent of my knowledge. I was sorely tempted to act like I knew, but I figured he'd see through that, and he was already mad at me. And I still needed to get enough information from him to complete the forms in a way that would satisfy my supervisor, who was a bit of a stickler for detail.

So I braced myself and told him the truth. "Well, the truth is I don't really know what a panic attack is. But wait!," I said, as he got up to leave. "You need me to sign these papers so you can get your medication, right?" He nodded, the way you might to encourage a child to explain about a broken lamp. "Well," I said, "if you'll stay here and teach me some about panic attacks, I'll sign your papers and we'll both be happy."

He did. He gave me an earful. Later, my supervisor gave me an earful as well, because I spent so much time on one intake. But it was worth it, because that was the start of my education about panic disorder. While I'd like to be able to say that he came back to see me and I was able to help him get off his medication and resume a full active life, unfortunately, I never saw him again. He got me interested in panic, though, and that started me on a career path that that's been immensely satisfying—helping people recover from panic attacks. So if you're out there reading this, sir, thanks for helping me get started.

My approach is largely based on cognitive behavioral treatment (CBT) methods. CBT is generally considered to be the treatment of choice for panic and anxiety disorders. But all too often, when people try to use CBT on their own in a self-help format, they get disappointing results. I think the reason is that they think of the CBT methods as a form of protection from panic, and try to use them that way. Using CBT methods, or anything else, to protect yourself from panic only serves to perpetuate the panic trick. In this book, I will show you how to avoid that common mistake, how to defuse the panic trick, and get the results you seek.

Many of my suggestions may make you think, "I never would have thought of doing that," or "That's pretty much the opposite of what I've been doing!" You may raise your eyebrows or even laugh out loud at a suggestion that seems surprising or bizarre. That's usually a good sign. If you keep thinking, and acting, the same way you did before reading this book, you're likely to stay the same. My job is to promote positive change.

So sometimes I may ask you a "dumb question." Sometimes I may ask you to do or think about things that you would rather avoid. Sometimes I'll ask you to try an experiment that seems really silly. Sometimes I'll ask questions that may seem blunt or insensitive. In short, sometimes I may say and do things that would be considered rude or odd in a friendship or other kind of social relationship. That's because I'm trying to help you find your way out of the panic trick.

I mention this because my approach may sometimes feel unsettling because I'm challenging you to think about things in a different way. Don't make snap judgments, and don't be in a hurry. When you have a strong reaction to something I've written here, it probably indicates an opportunity for change, and a good time to check out all your assumptions.

A person with chronic panic attacks and phobias needs to think and act differently in order to recover. If nothing in this book challenges or confronts or confuses you, if you instantly agree with everything I've written, without reservation or apprehension, then either you've already achieved a good recovery, or I haven't written a very useful book.

But if you focus with me on the phenomena of panic attacks and phobias, I'll show you how they work, how they trick you, why you have them, and, most importantly, what you can do to get over them and regain your freedom.

You won't find anything about medication in this book. Medication can be helpful to some people, but that's not what this book is about. I'm going to show you how you can recover from panic attacks and live happily and freely *without* medications.

You can recover from panic attacks and phobias. Hope to see you at the mall, on the expressway, or in the airport!

How to Use This Book

This book is organized into four sections. The first is an introduction, designed to help orient you to the approach I use, and guide you through some preliminary steps before starting to work.

Part One will help you understand precisely what the panic trick is, how it works, and most importantly, help you find evidence of it in your own life and behavior so you can begin undoing it. The "work" part of the workbook starts in this section, where I ask you to do some writing and complete some tasks, and continues throughout the rest of the book.

Part Two shows you how to prepare the way for recovery. It introduces a number of ways you can make yourself a better candidate for recovery, and make success more likely, even before you start the desensitization and exposure part of the program.

Part Three details how to design and use your own desensitization and exposure program for panic attacks and phobias.

Part Four offers additional detail and methods for overcoming four phobias commonly associated with panic attacks—the fears of flying, public speaking, driving, and claustrophobia, and the related disorder of social phobia.

This book is packed with ideas and suggestions. Most of them are counterintuitive, the opposite of what you might suppose, so there's a lot to think about and absorb. Here are a few suggestions to help make your work productive.

1. Read, don't skim, a chapter at a time. If you don't have enough time to read a complete chapter, and complete the exercises in it, plan a time when you can, and wait until then. Don't read small sections of this book "on the fly." That would probably give you enough information to make you anxious, but not enough to develop a plan.

2. Do each exercise as it comes up. If you're a perfectionist, or if you notice you keep putting the exercises off for a better time, or when you're "in the mood," recognize this for what it is—anxiety and procrastination—and allow yourself to do an imperfect job now. Better done than perfect.

3. Have a comfortable place in which to do your reading and writing, relatively free of noise and distraction.

4. Don't engage in other activities while you work with this book. No eating, radio or television in the background, or watching kids.

5. Expect that you will feel anxious. It involves a difficult topic for you, and it would be strange if you didn't feel any anxiety about it. Accept your feelings, and do the reading and exercises as best you can at that time.

PART ONE

UNMASKING THE TRICK

1
....

Panic Attacks and You

I recommend you take four steps before starting the work described in this book.

Step 1. See if you have the kind of problem that this book is designed to help.

Step 2. Consult with your physician.

Step 3. Consult a mental health professional.

Step 4. Enlist the aid of a "buddy."

Step 1: See if You Have the Kind of Problem that This Book Is Designed to Help

Panic attacks and phobias are the predominant feature in four anxiety disorders. They are:

- Panic disorder without agoraphobia
- Panic disorder with agoraphobia
- Specific phobia
- Social phobia.

If you have **panic disorder** (with or without agoraphobia), a **specific phobia**, or **social phobia** (or social anxiety disorder, as it's also known), this book has been written expressly for you. It may provide all the strategy and methods you need, or at least provide what you need to make a lot of progress toward recovery.

If you have panic attacks and phobias as part of a disorder other than the ones listed above, the discussion and methods in this book will still be helpful to you in learning how to handle the panic and phobias. You will probably need additional materials and/or professional help to manage the other aspects of the disorder. If you have panic disorder and some other disorder as well, this book will help you with the panic, and you'll need to find additional help for whatever else troubles you.

To make an initial determination whether you suffer from one of the disorders this book is designed to help, fill out the following questionnaire. Of course, a reliable diagnosis can only come from a visit to a trained mental health professional. We'll get into that shortly. This questionnaire is designed for adults and adolescents 16 and older.

Self-Assessment

1. Place a check mark beside each of the following symptoms you have experienced that developed abruptly and reached a peak within ten minutes:

❑ palpitations, pounding heart, or accelerated heart rate

❑ sweating

❑ trembling or shaking

❑ sensations of shortness of breath or smothering

❑ feeling of choking

❑ chest pain or discomfort

❑ nausea or abdominal distress

❑ feeling dizzy, unsteady, lightheaded, or faint

❑ derealization (feelings of unreality) or depersonalization (being detached from oneself)

❑ fear of losing control or going crazy

❑ fear of dying

❑ paresthesia (numbness or tingling sensations)

❑ chills or hot flushes

❑ other _____

A panic attack is defined as a discrete period of intense fear or discomfort, in which four (or more) of the above symptoms developed abruptly and reached a peak within ten minutes. With this definition in mind, look at which symptoms you have checked above. Have you experienced one or more panic attacks?

❑ Yes   ❑ No

2. In all your experience with panic, have you had at least two panic attacks that came "out of the blue." In other words, were these attacks you did not expect or anticipate because you were not in any kind of situation you usually feared?

❑ Yes   ❑ No

(If "no," go directly to 7. You don't appear to meet the criteria for panic disorder.)

3. Did one or more of these panic attacks change your usual attitude and behavior for at least one month, in one or more of the following ways?

  a. worry about having additional attacks

  b. worry about what an attack implies about you (for example, "going crazy") or might do to you (for example, heart attack or loss of control)

  c. a significant change in your behavior because of the attacks, and fears of more attacks

  ❏ Yes   ❏ No

  (If "no," you don't appear to meet the criteria for panic disorder; go directly to 7. If "yes," you appear to meet the criteria for panic disorder; check "panic disorder" in the space below 15, then proceed to 4.)

4. Do you avoid going into certain situations, or engaging in certain activities, in an effort to avoid having another panic attack?

  ❏ Yes   ❏ No

5. Are there situations or activities in which you will participate only if you can try to prevent a panic attack by bringing either a trusted companion, or certain objects that reassure you, such as a cellular phone or a water bottle?

  ❏ Yes   ❏ No

6. If you do not avoid any situations or activities, are there activities or situations in which you experience a great deal of anxiety and fear about having a panic attack?

  ❏ Yes   ❏ No

  *(If you answered "yes" to any one of questions 4, 5, and 6, you appear to meet the criteria for **panic disorder with agoraphobia**. If you answered "no" to all three questions, you appear to meet the criteria for **panic disorder without agoraphobia**. Go to 15 and check the appropriate box, then proceed to 7.)*

7. Do you experience a strong, persistent fear of situations in which:

  a. you are exposed to unfamiliar people

  b. you receive attention from others

  c. you make some kind of presentation or performance for an audience

  ❏ Yes   ❏ No

8. Do you fear that you will act in an embarrassing or humiliating way in these situations?

  ❏ Yes   ❏ No

  (If you answered "yes" to both 7 and 8, proceed to 9. If you answered "no" to one or both, go directly to 13 because you don't appear to meet the criteria for social phobia.)

9. Do you avoid such situations in order to avoid the anxiety?

   ❑ Yes   ❑ No

10. Do you become highly anxious when you are actually in such a situation?

    ❑ Yes   ❑ No

    (If you answered "yes" to either 9 or 10, proceed to 11. If you answered "no" to both, go directly to 13, because you don't appear to meet the criteria for social phobia.)

11. Do you have responses to social situations, and the anxiety you experience about them, which interfere significantly with:

a. your normal routine	❑ Yes	❑ No
b. your work or school performance	❑ Yes	❑ No
c. your social activities	❑ Yes	❑ No
d. your mood in general	❑ Yes	❑ No

(If you answered "yes" to at least one of them, proceed to 12. If you answered "no" to all four, go directly to 13, because you don't appear to meet the criteria for social phobia.)

12. Do your fears include a wide variety of social situations, or are they focused on just one or two areas, such as public speaking and introducing yourself at meetings? (Check only one.)

   ❑ a. a wide variety

   ❑ b. just one or two areas

   *(If you selected "a," you appear to meet criteria for **social phobia, generalized type**. If you selected "b," you appear to meet criteria for a **social phobia, specific type**. Go to 15 and check the appropriate box, then proceed to 13.)*

13. Do you fear and avoid any fairly specific situation or object, such as:

   ❑ certain animals or insects (for example, spiders, bees, dogs, birds, snakes, etc.)

   ❑ storms, or aspects of storms such as thunder, lightning, wind, etc.

   ❑ heights

   ❑ water

   ❑ darkness

   ❑ blood or injuries

   ❑ injections and the equipment used for injections

   ❑ medical procedures

   ❑ doctors or dentists

   ❑ illnesses

❏ bridges

❏ tunnels

❏ flying

❏ elevators

❏ driving

❏ enclosed spaces

❏ vomiting

❏ choking

❏ other _____

(If you checked at least one, proceed to 14. If you didn't check any, go directly to 15. You don't appear to meet criteria for specific phobia.)

14. Do you experience this fear only when you have to face the situation you fear, or think about it? Or do you experience it in situations that are entirely unconnected? (Check only one.)

❏ a. only when I face it or think about it

❏ b. could be anytime, anyplace

*(If you checked "a," you appear to meet the criteria for **specific phobia**; go to 15, check the box for specific phobia, and list your feared situations or objects in that section. If you checked "b," go on to 15 without marking any more boxes, because you don't appear to meet the criteria for specific phobia.)*

15. **Results of my self-assessment:**

Panic disorder

❏ with agoraphobia

❏ without agoraphobia

Social phobia

❏ generalized type

❏ specific type

Specific phobia (identify feared objects or locations)

_____

_____

_____

Your self-assessment indicates that you meet criteria for the anxiety disorders you checked above. There are still some steps you need to take in order to establish a conclusive diagnosis. These steps are explained in the rest of this chapter. Feel free to read the rest of this section if you are curious, but when you are ready, move on to Step 2 of this chapter.

If you haven't checked any of the items above, it means you don't appear to meet criteria for any of the disorders this book is most concerned with.

What do you do now?

You might be experiencing another anxiety disorder, one that is not the principal focus of this book. I suggest you next take a look at a self-assessment questionnaire that screens for all anxiety disorders. There's one at the website of the Anxiety Disorders Association of America. Check the Resources at the end of the book for the address.

If you do have another anxiety disorder, there might still be parts of this book that are useful for you, depending on what it is. Complete the broader assessment first, then come back and take a look. If it turns out that you experience another anxiety disorder that includes significant panic attacks, such as posttraumatic stress disorder, you can use the methods in this book to help overcome the attacks. If you have generalized anxiety disorder, a problem characterized by chronic worry rather than panic, you might find some help in the chapter on worry, and the material on working with anxious thoughts.

No need to be alarmed if you didn't fit into one of the categories here. This book is principally for people who have panic attacks and phobias. If you have some other kind of problem, or suspect you do, be sure to discuss your needs with a mental health professional, and seek his or her advice on the suitability of this book for your purposes.

Step 2: Consult with Your Physician

Everyone who experiences panic attacks should have one good physical after the panic attacks begin in order to rule out the possibility, slim though it is, that your panic attacks are caused by a physical disorder. There are a number of possibilities, none of them very common, including disorders of the heart, thyroid, and adrenal glands.

Make written notes of what you want to discuss with your physician before you call for an appointment. The doctor's staff will probably ask you why you want an appointment; tell them that you've been having some problems and briefly summarize them.

Avoiding the Doctor: A Common Problem

People commonly fear (and avoid) going to the doctor, for a variety of reasons. If you are claustrophobic, you may fear waiting in a small examination room. You may be afraid you'll have a panic attack while waiting for the doctor; you may be afraid of hearing "bad news" from

> *I once worked with a woman whose fear of the dentist centered on seeing his white coat, so we arranged for him to wear street clothes for her first visit. Once she felt more comfortable with him, his wardrobe ceased to be an issue.*

Suggestions for Doctor Visits

- Ask to be seen first or last, for shorter times waiting in the examination room
- Take several measures of blood pressure throughout the visit, in the knowledge that it will go down as you get used to being there
- Have a glass of water available
- Ask that a staff member to check in on you while you wait for the doctor
- Have a support person with you.

may regularly experience a rise in blood pressure on visiting the doctor, and fear the doctor or his/her staff will exaggerate its importance. You may fear the doctor will become impatient with your complaints, or think you are odd. You may fear the doctor will insist that you take medication. Or you may be afraid of needles and the sight of blood.

Hiding these fears and trying to "tough it out" almost always makes the anxiety worse. So if these fears discourage you from visiting the doctor, here's what I suggest. When you call for the appointment, speak with the nurse or office manager and tell that person you have difficulty with doctor visits because of anxiety. Explain briefly what your concern is; and ask them to help make it easier for you.

Beyond the specifics of these arrangements, it can be very helpful to know that the doctor is aware of your anxiety, and that you can talk about it, rather than try to hide it and fight it. The effort to hide and fight your anxiety is usually the most significant obstacle to recovery.

People often worry that the doctor won't want to be bothered or that the doctor's staff will find their concerns ridiculous. People with panic disorder generally find that the doctor is more understanding than they expected. But if you find that your doctor really lacks the patience to help you sort through this trouble, find another doctor.

What to Expect from Your Physician

The reason to visit your physician is to rule out any physical ailments; your physician is not an expert in mental health. However, your physician should listen to your symptoms, review your history, ask questions, run appropriate tests, and offer feedback and recommendations.

There are numerous physical conditions that can produce panic symptoms, and your physician should evaluate you for those possibilities if that has never been done before. They include hyperthyroidism, hypoglycemia, anemia, mitral valve prolapse, asthma, and vertigo, among others. However, if you have already had a thorough examination and your doctor assured you that you were in good health, *do not push for continual retesting.* You can waste lots of time and money that way.

Physicians often expect you will be pleased if the test results indicate that you have no physical ailments. However, my experience is that people with panic attacks are often dismayed to hear those words, "you're in good health," because it suggests to them that the physician simply didn't find the ailment they believe, or even hope, they have. People with panic attacks often hope to find a physical ailment, even a serious disease, because they don't want to think they have a "psychological" or "mental" problem.

The purpose of the consultation with your physician is to shed light on what you have and don't have, not to find the disease of your choice. If it turns out you have panic attacks, this book will help you solve the problem.

If your physician finds evidence of a physical ailment, then you should proceed to get treatment for that ailment, and defer working on the panic until you see how that treatment progresses. However, if your physician cheerily congratulates you on being "in excellent health," briefly feel your disappointment and move on to Step 3.

Step 3: Consult a Mental Health Professional

I think this book will enable a lot of people to recover on their own, without regular visits to a mental health professional. Others will need regular treatment sessions to help them achieve the recovery they want. I think the best way to see

When You Need Therapy

If you experience other significant difficulties in life in addition to panic attacks and phobias, you would do well to discuss those with a mental health professional before embarking on the work described in this book. There are some problems that need to be resolved first, before you can expect to benefit from the methods described herein. For instance, if you are presently dependent on alcohol or drugs, you need to make some progress in that area before you do this work. Otherwise, you will probably continue to make use of those substances to "self medicate" the anxiety, and that will block your progress.

If you presently feel "trapped" in a very bad marriage, where substance abuse and/or physical and mental abuse is a factor, you probably need to tackle that problem simultaneously with the panic attacks, if not before. Panic attacks associated with living with an abusive spouse, or one whose addiction to drugs or alcohol causes severe family strife, will probably not be completely dispelled by the methods described in this book.

If you are severely depressed, and the depression appeared *before* the panic attacks, you may need to first get some help with the depression before you can make progress with the panic attacks.

Choosing the Right Mental Health Professional

You have a number of choices in selecting a mental health professional:

- psychiatrists
- psychologists
- clinical social workers
- other types of counselors

There are differences in the training and licensing requirements among these professions, and choosing among them can seem complicated. I don't want to complicate your job here, so I'm going to offer you some simple advice on selecting one. Not everyone will agree with my advice, and you should assume it reflects my own personal biases as a psychologist.

Psychiatrists are physicians who specialize in mental health. They generally use medication as their treatment method, because that is their area of speciality. Because the odds are high that a psychiatrist will recommend medication to you, and will probably be much less familiar with cognitive behavioral methods than will other practitioners, I suggest you select one of the other professions for your initial consultation. Of course, if you want medication, you should go directly to a psychiatrist.

Which other profession? I think this is less important than finding a professional who truly has some specialized training and experience with the cognitive behavioral treatment of panic. In major urban areas, such people are generally available, if you know how to look. In rural areas, unfortunately, there are often none.

For referral sources to help you find a qualified professional, see Resources (page 236). You will also find resources listed on my website, www.anxietycoach.com.

which method will work for you is to try the least intrusive, least expensive way first, which would be the self-help method contained in this book. Work it hard for three months, and then evaluate the results you're getting.

Even if you decide that you are going to work on your own, I do suggest that everyone who experiences difficulty with panic attacks have one consultation with a good mental health practitioner who is familiar with the cognitive behavioral treatment of panic attacks. Evaluating your situation with a professional who has worked with people in your situation will help clarify the particular kind of anxiety disorder you are experiencing, and may enable you to target your efforts more precisely. You might get useful feedback from that session that you can employ in your own recovery work. At worst, if nothing useful comes from it, at least you can approach your self-help work with a clear mind, knowing you left no stone unturned.

Step 4: Enlist the Aid of a "Buddy"

It will be a big help to have someone with whom you can discuss your efforts on a regular basis. You can think of such a person as a buddy, a coach, a confidant, a sponsor in the Alcoholics Anonymous sense of the word, or a support person. They don't have to be an expert, although they should do a little reading to inform themselves, perhaps reading this book, or reading some of the material on my website. They just need to be somebody you know is in your corner.

A major benefit is that, by telling your buddy of your efforts, you will find it easier to monitor your progress and hold yourself accountable. It's easy to forget about all your good intentions when you keep them to yourself.

I'm not talking here about the traditional "support person," who often accompanies people with panic disorder as they venture into areas they usually avoid, although these two roles could be combined under the right circumstances. I'm talking here about someone you might chat with on a regular basis, maybe 15 minutes a week or so, just to have a forum to review and report on your work and progress. The purpose here isn't to report to someone so they can check on you. It's to have a regularly scheduled report time to make it more likely that *you* will check on you.

. . . or a Good Support Group

A good anxiety/panic support group can be a great help in your recovery work. The trick is to find a good one, because these groups vary enormously in their quality and effectiveness.

For a discussion of support groups, and suggestions of how to find one in your community, see Resources in the back of this book.

2
....

The Experience of Panic Attacks

Everyone who experiences panic attacks has their own distinct story to tell, and often thinks that they suffer from a bizarre problem which is all their own. Yet they all share some major aspects.

Audrey is a fairly typical example of a person experiencing panic disorder. She was in her mid-40s when she first came to see me. She had lived in Chicago all her life, and had scarcely been outside the city in all that time. She had been completely housebound during the worst of it and was still extremely limited in what she could do when she came to me for treatment. She had the brains, the energy, the enthusiasm and the ambition to succeed in a variety of professions, but worked part-time as a gardener because that enabled her to avoid the situations she feared. Those situations included highway driving, being more than a few minutes from the "safety" of home, riding in buses, trains, or airplanes, and shopping in crowded stores or malls.

Audrey's first panic attack occurred at age 32, while she was driving alone on one of the highways that span Chicago. She suddenly felt warm and flushed. Although she tried not to pay much attention to it, she found herself wondering if she was going to pass out. She told herself that was "crazy" but it didn't help. She started to sweat, felt like she couldn't catch her breath, and felt her heart race. She wondered if she were still in her body, or floating outside of it somehow. Fearing that she was losing her mind, she turned the car around and raced home.

She didn't tell anybody at first. She didn't know what to say, and she feared sounding foolish. But from that day forward, fearing a repetition of the experience, she avoided driving outside of a small "safety zone" around her home if at all possible.

Over time, she became apprehensive about any situation from which a quick exit might be difficult in the event of a panic attack. She started shopping at the 24-hour supermarket late at night, when there were no lines at the cash register.

After a while, even that seemed too risky, because there were so many places from which she couldn't see the exit, so she restricted herself to convenience stores. As her list of places to avoid grew, she saw less and less of her friends, becoming isolated and making excuses not to go outside of her home. For about four months she didn't leave her home at all. She grew depressed about the way her life had been disrupted, especially during this housebound time.

Before she came to me, Audrey saw therapists who wanted to review her childhood memories for clues to her fears, and others who suggested that her panic was an excuse to avoid activities for some unknown reason. Some sternly refused to discuss her panic attacks, insisting instead that she focus on the "underlying reasons" for them, although it was never clear what these reasons were. She saw psychiatrists who put her on medications and physicians who ran numerous tests seeking a physical cause for her trouble. She got little relief from any of them.

Audrey carried a water bottle wherever she went, thinking that a drink of water would somehow interrupt her panic attack. Most of the year, she kept the air conditioning on in the car, believing that the cool air would help. She avoided commitments to be anywhere at a fixed time with the words "I'll see how I feel," or "let's talk again when the time gets closer."

Audrey became caught up in the classic "fear of fear itself." She feared that anxiety would lead to a panic attack, which she thought would kill her or make her crazy. She tried desperately to prevent herself from becoming nervous—and, of course, that made her more anxious than ever.

After working hard with the cognitive behavioral methods I describe in this book, Audrey made an excellent recovery. The first time Audrey drove far enough out of the city that she saw, for the first time in her life, a cow in a pasture, she was so excited you'd think she had seen a dinosaur. With her excitement came a powerful pride that she was finally winning back her freedom. She now drives anywhere she wants, including lengthy cross country trips. She goes to her job outside the home every day. She no longer feels ashamed of her troubles. Once in a while she feels a twinge of anxiety, remembering her past panic attacks, but then she simply tells herself, "I don't do that anymore." It's hard to appreciate what a powerful experience it is for a person like Audrey to get over this problem. She was literally enslaved by panic, and now she's free.

Audrey's story describes a case of full-blown panic disorder with agoraphobia. Outside her narrow safety zone, she came to fear just about everything. But phobias can also be very specific. A person may fear one narrowly defined object or circumstance, such as dogs or elevators. People with these phobias *aren't usually afraid of what the object will do to them.* They're afraid that their reaction to the object will be so disproportionate, so out of control, that they will suffer permanent harm or disgrace as a result.

The Lobster Tale

I worked with a woman who had a lifelong fear of lobsters. She wasn't afraid that a lobster would bite her. In fact, she was just as afraid of a cooked lobster on a tray as of a live one. Her fear was the classical *fear of fear*. She feared that she would become so afraid in the presence of a lobster that she would lose control of herself and suffer irreparable harm as a result. Maybe she would react so wildly to the sight of a lobster in a restaurant that she would have a heart attack. Maybe she would run out the door and across the street, and in so doing, get hit by a car. Maybe in her panicked exit she would knock over and injure innocent parties. Her worst fear was that she would become so afraid as to go insane.

She had the same kind of fears about her fear as does a person with panic disorder. She differed only in the respect that her panic was exclusively triggered by lobsters.

Of course, if you don't have a fear of lobsters, it's almost incomprehensible how this could be a big problem, especially when you're living in a landlocked state. But when you're afraid of losing your mind in the presence of a lobster, and when you're just as afraid of a cooked one, or a picture of one, as of a live specimen, then it will seem to you that they could be anywhere.

And so even a fear that otherwise appears to be amusing can literally deprive you of your freedom. That's what it did to Gail, who called herself "lobster girl" in mocking reference to the presence of this unusual fear in an otherwise perfectly normal life. She and her family had to restrict their vacations to landlocked sites. Her husband, who regularly entertained business clients over dinner, had to scout restaurants in advance when the spouses would attend, to ensure an absence of lobsters on the menu. She had to check with a good friend before seeing a movie, in order to avoid any films that had lobster scenes. She read magazines hesitantly, ready to pitch them away should she turn the page to see a photo of a lobster. She knew that none of it made sense, but that didn't help.

In discussing the fear she felt at the grocery store, which had a lobster tank in the corner, she told me this:

"I stand in the front of the store and watch people—men, women, children, older couples—and I see them walk by the lobster tank, as if it were nothing. And I ask myself, 'How do they do that?'"

After more than 20 years of this exquisite torture, Gail saw me for a few months, during which we worked the methods I describe in this book. As frightened and ashamed of her fear as she was, she wouldn't even tell me what scared her when we first spoke on the phone. Yet in this relatively short period of time, she completely overcame her fear. Imagine what a relief it is to be freed of this burden. For years afterward, I received postcards from her on vacation. They were always from coastal sites like New Orleans, Boston, and San Francisco. The cards always had a photo of a fish market or a table full of lobsters, and a little note on the back that said "I picked this card out all by myself!"

Audrey and Gail represent two distinctive experiences with panic attacks and phobias. Parts of the story are always the same, and other parts always different. The general experience with panic attacks and phobias is something like this.

In the Beginning: The First Attack

If you're developing panic disorder, the first attack is usually an unexpected experience, something that occurs, as people say, "out of the blue."

You're going along, minding your own business. Maybe you're shopping in a busy grocery store; or driving on a highway; or waiting at a red light on a hot day; or sitting in church trying to follow along with the sermon, but your mind keeps wandering. Maybe you're on vacation somewhere nice, but far from home. Maybe you're even home in bed, sound asleep.

The next thing you know, you feel some terrible symptoms, for no apparent reason. Maybe your heart races, or seems exceptionally loud. You might feel hot and sweaty, dizzy or lightheaded, have trouble breathing, feel chest pain or tightness, feel numb or tingly in your extremities, feel weak in your legs. You might experience a strange sense of unreality, as if you don't know if you're there in your body, or floating around somewhere. And you feel really afraid. You might not know exactly why, but you're really afraid.

That's the general picture, although the details will vary. Some people get a few moments of preliminary symptoms before the attack arrives full blown, and some don't. People get different combinations of symptoms, too. The panic attacks you have won't be the same as someone else's. Nor will each of yours be identical. You might find that they change over time, as different symptoms come to your attention.

Making Sense of the First Attack

The physical symptoms are powerful and dramatic, so it's no wonder that they lead people to think they're dying, or experiencing some other calamity such as fainting, having a "nervous breakdown," or just losing control of themselves in all kinds of ways.

It's very important to notice that *these thoughts of catastrophe are also symptoms of a panic attack*. They're not clear and accurate warnings of danger. They're symptoms of anxiety. They're simply the thoughts that you usually have when you get afraid.

Text continued on page 30.

Why People Develop Panic Attacks and Phobias

People with panic and phobias usually want very much to know "why" they have panic attacks, and frequently ask themselves that question. "Why me?" they'll ask themselves, again and again. "Why here? Why now?"

It's perfectly natural to want to know why you have panic. But first I want to tell you that the "why" questions won't be all that useful to you. In fact, focusing on the "why" questions is much more likely to get you stuck than it is to help you recover.

When people ask themselves the "why" question, they're not really looking for information. They're usually getting mad at themselves. That anger isn't going to be part of the solution.

I see two general patterns in the history of people who come to me for help with fears and phobias.

The first type is people who can trace their phobias directly back to childhood, without interruption. Whatever they fear, be it public speaking, flying, an insect or other animal, or whatever, their history shows that they have always been afraid of it. These are childhood phobias that were never outgrown. They are most likely to be specific phobias rather than phobias associated with panic disorder. Generally, people who have this kind of history with their fear are much less concerned with the "why" question. They tend to see it as a fear that's always, or almost always, been with them, so they don't see much mystery about it.

The second pattern is much more likely to be associated with panic disorder, and gives rise to much more preoccupation with the "why?" question. In this case, people can look back to a time in their life when they *didn't* have the phobia they have now. In fact, they often can recall a time in their life when they thoroughly enjoyed the activity or situation they now fear, or when they felt "fearless" in general.

For instance, a fearful flyer will rarely be a person who has never flown in his life. Most are people who flew, and in many cases flew quite frequently, before they became afraid. Some were pilots in the military, and loved it. It's pretty much the same with people who fear driving. They generally had years of driving experience before becoming phobic.

For these people, the "why" question bothers them like a burning saddle burr. They see their life divided into two different parts—the part before they developed panic attacks, and the part after. They liked the first part a lot better. And they ask, "Why?"

There are three basic reasons.

The first is that there is almost certainly a genetic predisposition to panic attacks and phobias. Some people are born likely to develop panic attacks under the right circumstances, and some people couldn't have a panic attack if you paid them. There isn't anything unusual about this. I think we will eventually find out that most people have an inborn tendency to respond to stress and change in one particular way or another. If you have panic attacks, this is yours.

Other people have different tendencies than you. Some of them are prone to high blood pressure, excessive drinking or use of drugs, or nail-biting and hair-pulling. Nobody got to choose.

A second reason has to do with the circumstances and atmosphere of their childhood. Adults with panic disorder seem to have often grown up in an atmosphere that, for one reason or another, failed to teach them the world was a safe place where they could happily pursue their own enjoyment. Perhaps, had circumstances been different, their predisposition to panic would have remained dormant. But it didn't turn out that way. Maybe there was an early death in the family, severe illness, or some other serious problem such as alcoholism. It could have been the opposite kind of problem—maybe the parents were themselves anxious and overprotective, and this unwittingly strengthened the child's sense of vulnerability. Or perhaps the child learned to spend too much time and effort taking care of others, trying too hard to please them, and feeling responsible for their happiness.

The third reason has to do with the stress of becoming an independent adult. For most people who develop panic attacks, it begins in their twenties or thirties—the years of establishing an independent life for yourself when you are most likely to experience these kinds of changes. This is more likely than anything else to answer questions about why you're afraid of flying or driving now, even though for a number of years you drove and flew without a problem.

What these three reasons have in common is that none of them was under your own control. They are developmental events in life, not something you can choose. There is no reason to feel guilty for or ashamed of having panic attacks. If you have panic attacks, that's your problem to solve or leave unsolved. But don't get fooled into thinking it is your fault.

This is where the trick of panic begins, when you try and make sense of the experience, and begin having these catastrophic thoughts. The catastrophic thoughts, in turn, lead to more physical symptoms, and so it goes.

For most phobics, the ultimate fear is of losing control of themselves…as a result of their fear.

Responses to the First Attack

People usually flee the scene of their first attack, often without attracting any attention. If they're indoors, they'll usually exit the building, and might feel some relief as soon as they reach the outside. If they're in a car and unable to park and leave immediately, they're liable to open the windows or turn on the air conditioning and feel some relief from the movement of air. They may go away to a private place to "get a hold of themselves," or might go to the emergency room of a hospital.

If the attack takes place at work, or somewhere else in the company of others, their friends or family may insist on taking them to an emergency room or calling the paramedics. This attention from others who want to help is often the source of additional discomfort, and leads the person to try and hide any future attacks from others. If they became panicky in the midst of a social situation, like a party or a meeting, they are liable to make an excuse and leave. Less frequently, they ask for help, but all too often, the help they get isn't all that helpful.

People who go to the emergency room with their first panic attack often have an unsatisfactory experience. They often get a general message from the staff that "there is nothing wrong with them," and that they should go home and relax. Of course, there is something wrong. The person had a panic attack. **It's not that there's nothing wrong, but that the thing that's wrong isn't dangerous.** This distinction, unfortunately, often gets lost in the discussion.

Prelude to an Attack

There are some typical patterns to the onset of panic disorder. A first attack most often occurs when one is between the ages of 18–35, and often follows a period of significant changes associated with becoming an independent adult, in such major areas of life as work, residence, family, finances, and health. The first panic attack often follows:

- taking a first full-time job
- moving away from home
- buying a home
- getting married
- having children.

Panic onset can also be a response to a long period of difficulty, such as:

- severe depression
- feeling "trapped" in a bad marriage or other situation
- the death of a loved one
- prolonged stress associated with long periods of uncertainty about one's health, career, or financial well-being.

But it doesn't take bad events to get panic disorder going. In fact, people frequently develop panic attacks when everything seems to be going well in their life and they're starting to attain their personal goals. This often puzzles them because they assume that panic would only come if they were having terrible troubles. Not so. Panic attacks can develop when you experience a lot of change in a small period of time, even if it's all welcome change.

The Riddle of Panic

One of the peculiarities of a panic attack is that it typically subsides and ends without harming the person or causing any of the calamities they fear. I'm sure you've heard this before. I mention it not because I expect it to relieve your fears but because it can reveal an important aspect of panic.

Why does that happen? Since people with panic disorder don't get crippled, killed, or driven mad by the panic attacks, why do they continue to be afraid of them? Why don't people eventually catch on and lose their fear without having to make any particular effort?

This is a terribly important point, and I will return to it in Chapter 5.

Demoralization

The days and weeks after a first panic attack are often a demoralizing experience. It's not enough that you just went through a terrifying experience in which you thought you were dying or going crazy. You may also have encounters with physicians and other professional helpers who aren't well prepared to respond to this kind of problem. At best, they may treat you kindly, and suggest you seek out a therapist or take some medication. At worse, they may be dismissive of a problem for which they're not trained, and inclined to suggest that you just "get over it" or relax with a cup of tea and forget about it. But a person who fears death and insanity will not be cured by a cup of tea, or even a warm bath.

Your friends and family are probably also unprepared to be helpful, unless they have some personal experience with panic themselves. They may try their best to help you but find that they just don't know how, and you may feel frustrated and unsupported.

Avoidance and Anticipation

You probably find that you worry about having another panic attack, and struggle to get rid of those thoughts, without success. You may already be making subtle changes in your daily routine in an effort to avoid another panic attack—for example, avoiding the site where the first panic attack occurred. Your sleep, appetite, and sense of well-being may be seriously disrupted in the aftermath of a first attack.

The Panic Cycle

Most people who have one attack will have more. There are a number of reasons for this, but one big one is that they emerge from the initial experience confused, demoralized, and worried about their future. This leads them to think and act in ways that they hope will "protect" them, but only make future attacks more likely. And then they get caught up in a spiral of fearful anticipation of panic attacks; efforts to protect themselves by avoidance and other responses that disrupt their life; and more attacks.

This is the main reason so many people come to grief when they try to protect themselves from their anxiety. They tell themselves "don't think about it"; they resist it; they try somehow to force themselves to feel better; they get angry at themselves; they feel shame and embarrassment about feeling anxious; they try to keep it a secret from others; and they try to medicate it away with alcohol, nicotine, and other substances.

These all make the anxiety worse.

It's not simply that "resistance is futile." It's that resisting anxiety fuels the fears. Struggling against fear is like putting out fires with gasoline.

Fortunately, there is a way out for people with panic attacks, whether the attacks are part of panic disorder, social phobia, specific phobias, or some other anxiety disorder. This way out will work for those of you who just had a first panic attack last week, and for those who had their first attack twenty years ago. It will work for you whatever you fear—public speaking, parties, illness, highway driving, crowded stores, elevators, dogs, or whatever. You can recover from panic attacks and phobias.

In the rest of Part One, I'm going to help you develop a different view of how panic and phobias "work," one that's more accurate and realistic. It's a view that

Root Cause versus Solution

I worked with a woman who grew up with a very overprotective mother. She recalled that her mother was afraid to let her ride her bicycle without supervision, even after she had learned good safety habits, and even though it was the norm in her neighborhood for kids her age to ride without supervision. (Just to put it in context, this woman grew up in the 1940s and '50s, when this was the general rule). Her mother developed this solution. She kept a ring of talcum powder around the bicycle in the basement, so that her daughter couldn't move the bicycle without leaving a telltale mark in the powder. She would be punished if she moved the bicycle, and in this manner her mother tried to protect her from an accident.

My client was a very determined person, even as a young girl, and was not to be deterred. She became strong enough that she could lift the bicycle straight up into the air and carry it away without smudging the powder. Her mother never discovered her secret, and she was able to ride her bicycle to her heart's content.

But though her body had developed to the point where she could lift the bicycle, and then ride it for hours, her mind hadn't developed to the point where she could truly feel okay about what she was doing. Because she was put into a situation where she had to break the rules in order to ride a bicycle like the other kids, she developed a strong sense of guilt, an underlying idea that she was doing something wrong, and that she would be punished for it eventually. As she reached late adolescence, this developed into panic attacks that would occur whenever she ventured "too far" from home.

My client believed that this was her "root cause," and I pretty much agreed with her. She probably inherited a genetic predisposition to caution and worry from her mother's side of the family, and her experience with the bicycle seemed central to the activation of this predisposition. I think this was as clear an example of finding a "smoking gun" cause as one can generally expect.

But knowing this didn't stop her panic attacks. She knew why she had the first one, but that didn't bring the recurrent attacks to a halt. She didn't have the recurrent attacks because of her background and bicycle experience. She had the recurrent attacks because she kept getting tricked into trying to protect herself from them.

When she was able to undo that, she had a good recovery.

will enable you to overcome panic attacks, phobias, and to a lesser extent, worry and other manifestations of anxiety. It's a view that's very consistent with the rules that govern our internal world of thoughts, physical sensations, and emotions.

Then I'm going to show you how you can use that view to create your own recovery.

3

....

The True Nature of Panic Attacks

Let's do some work now that will shed some light on the true nature of panic attacks.

I don't ask you to do the following exercise lightly, because I know you might find it uncomfortable. You might find that just thinking about an attack produces uncomfortable feelings and symptoms in you. Don't struggle with those feelings. Instead, think of this exercise as one of the first steps toward your recovery. Practice experiencing the feelings, rather than avoiding or struggling against them.

People often have a hard time describing their thoughts and fears from a panic attack, because the panic is so disruptive of your attention and memory.

This approach often helps: Imagine that I could have spoken to you at the height of your panic, and asked you what you thought was about to happen to you. What would your answer have been at that time? Or if I could have literally heard a broadcast of your thoughts, as if they were going out on a radio show, while you were at the height of this panic attack, what specific thoughts would I have heard?

1. **First, briefly describe a panic attack you experienced, one that was a particularly powerful one, one that you remember clearly.** (The first one a person has is usually the worst, so use that one if you can recall it clearly.)

_____

_____

_____

_____

_____

_____

_____

_____

_____

2. **Take a few minutes now to recall what you feared was about to happen. Write your recollections here:**

_____

_____

_____

_____

_____

_____

The central fears of a panic attack are usually about some catastrophe, a change for the worse, that will turn out to be permanent. If you're like most people, you've probably experienced more than one kind of catastrophic fear.

1. **Identify several catastrophic fears you've experienced, and list them below. Be as specific as you can.**

_____

_____

_____

_____

_____

_____

2. **If you thought you were about to die, what did you think the cause of death would be?**

_____

_____

_____

3. If you thought you were about to act in an uncontrolled manner, what did you think you might do?

_____

_____

_____

_____

4. What did you think the consequences would be, to you and also to the people near you, and your friends and loved ones as well?

_____

_____

_____

_____

_____

5. If you feared you were going to faint, what did you think would happen next? And what did you think the consequences would be?

_____

_____

_____

_____

_____

_____

6. If you thought you were going to make a fool of yourself and lose people's respect and friendship, how did you fear they would treat you differently thereafter?

_____

_____

_____

_____

7. How would that affect your life?

_____

_____

_____

_____

8. Would the effects have been permanent or temporary?

_____

Now I want to ask you about what actually happened to you as a result of the panic attack. The feared outcomes you listed above, did they happen?

Since you're still here reading this, we know you didn't die, unless Shirley MacLaine is somehow involved. What about the other fears you had? Write down each fear you listed above and check off "yes" or "no" to show whether they happened.

FEAR	YES	NO
_____	❑	❑
_____	❑	❑
_____	❑	❑
_____	❑	❑
_____	❑	❑

Did you have any "yes" answers? If you did, you need to examine this further. For instance, if you fainted during a panic attack, with a full loss of consciousness, this requires further investigation. It's extremely rare to faint during a panic attack, so rare that if you actually faint, it's probably due to some other condition or circumstance so you should see a doctor.

On the other hand, if you *felt* like you were about to faint, but did not lose consciousness, that's another matter entirely. That's a very common symptom of panic. I'm asking about *what actually happened*, not how the attack made you feel, or what you think "almost" happened.

In the same way, if you vomited, and have a history of vomiting as a part of motion sickness, then you need to make some preparations for those times when you can realistically expect to vomit. But if you have a history of *feeling* like you would vomit, in the absence of a pattern of actually vomiting, then it would appear that you have the problem of a nervous stomach, and need to treat it as anxiety, not vomiting.

If you regularly vomit in a moving vehicle, talk to your doctor about treatment options and, until you get a good solution, keep a bag in your vehicle like the ones available on airplanes.

Sometimes people feel so confused and ashamed as a result of a panic attack that it affects the way they remember it. I recall a young woman who was horribly embarrassed by her memory of "kicking the door in" at her doctor's office when she had a panic attack in the waiting room. She eventually asked the receptionist about the incident, and discovered that not only was the original door still in place, without any sign of damage, but whatever she did was so mild that no one noticed. She then remembered that she had used her foot to prevent the door from swinging closed, but that's a far cry from "kicking in the door." So if your "yes" answer is that you did act in some uncontrolled way and humiliated yourself, I'd like to ask you a series of follow-up questions.

A good way to check the accuracy of your recollection is to look at the reactions of others.

1. Who was so offended or horrified that they now treat you differently?

_____

_____

_____

2. If you acted out of control in some important way, what were the consequences?

_____

_____

_____

3. Which of your friends, coworkers, and family will have nothing to do with you as a result of your behavior during the panic attack?

_____

_____

_____

Almost everybody's answer to questions 1 and 3 above is "no one" and "none." If your experience is different, I suggest you discuss it with a professional therapist.

Now I'm going to ask about the worst thing that ever happened to you because of a panic attack. Take a little time and think it over. Review some of the worst attacks you experienced. Other than scaring you terribly, what did it do to you?

But before you start writing, let me explain what I'm *not* asking for. Sometimes people reply by telling me what symptoms of fear they experienced, such as a racing heart, sweating, or hyperventilating. I know when a panic attack hits, you feel very afraid, but that's not what I'm asking about. I'm asking about what the panic attack actually *did* to you, not how scared you were or what form the fear took.

People often say things like "I nearly fainted" or "I felt like I was going to drive off the bridge." They think they just barely avoided a catastrophe, but now I'm not asking what you thought would happen. I want to know what actually *did* happen.

Don't rush through this.

What is the worst thing that ever happened to you as a result of a panic attack?

_____

_____

_____

_____

_____

If you're like most people with panic, you had trouble coming up with answers to this question. Most people can't really pinpoint anything that happened to them.

A panic attack is a horrible experience. It fills you with terrible fear. It convinces you that life as you knew it is over. But then it passes, and it turns out that very little happened. You feel embarrassed and apprehensive, but none of the terrible things you feared, such as death or insanity, actually happened to you.

Let's take this one step further. Any time you're dealing with concerns about your safety, you want to be thorough. You want to examine the question from all angles so you can know clearly whether you're in danger or not. When you thought you were about to experience such a catastrophe as death or insanity, and it did not occur, you may have developed a theory at the time as to why it didn't.

This next question is not rhetorical. If you think about it, you probably have some ideas as to why the catastrophe you feared didn't happen. Don't be concerned about whether or not the reasons seem like good ones. Write down all the reasons that have occurred to you, however logical or illogical they may be.

Why didn't you die, go crazy, or suffer the terrible outcomes you feared?

_____

_____

_____

_____

_____

In my experience, the one explanation people *don't* come up with is this: panic simply isn't capable of making those things happen. Most people continue to believe that they were actually at risk of dying or losing control and offer a variety of reasons why it didn't happen to them…yet.

Typical answers include: I didn't (die) (go crazy) (faint) (freak out) (strip my clothes off and knock people over in my rush out the door) or otherwise lose control of myself because:

1. I was lucky.
2. I left just in the nick of time.
3. I got distracted.
4. My spouse, or other "safe person," was with me.
5. I fought it off.
6. I had my children with me, and I knew I had to take care of them.
7. I called a friend on my cellular phone.
8. I had my water bottle with me and took a drink of cool water.
9. I remembered I had my Xanax with me and knew I could take it if I needed to.

Take a look at your reasons. Can any of them actually prevent death? Or insanity? Or uncontrolled misbehavior?

Most people attribute their survival in panic situations to factors that have nothing to do with safety or sanity. This is part of the panic trick. People attribute their survival to factors that didn't, and couldn't, save them. In this way, they overlook the fact that *nothing* really saved them. They didn't *need* to be saved, because they weren't in danger. They just got tricked into thinking they were.

What's worse, the kind of things that people assume kept them safe are very unreliable. When people attribute their survival to "luck," for instance, this actually makes them more and more anxious. Why? Because they figure luck is finite. They only have a limited supply. And they just used some up on this last panic attack. Soon, they'll run out of luck.

And so it goes with all the other reasons. What if my support person isn't there next time? What if I forget that old bottle of Xanax? What if my water bottle springs a leak? When you think that your survival depends on other people or objects, this makes you more anxious and less secure, because you worry that they might not be there the next time you need them.

This is terribly important. Noticing this major aspect of panic and learning how to use it will be a big step in your recovery. Panic only scares a person, nothing more. It seems to suggest something terrible is on the horizon, but the terrible thing never appears. It's a trick.

Sometimes people feel defensive about getting tricked. They feel criticized when it's pointed out. That's understandable. It may seem that, if someone says they were tricked, it's like calling them stupid. It's not, of course. Millions of smart, capable people get fooled by panic attacks. It's not that you're stupid. You get fooled because panic is a very effective trick.

Sometimes people so dislike the idea that they got tricked that they prefer believing that panic is dangerous, because that would mean they didn't get fooled. But this response, based on injured pride, tends to make people more stuck. Watch out for that kind of reaction. It can sabotage all your efforts.

This is a helpful first step in getting over panic attacks. It's not a cure. But it's one step of many toward recovery.

Questions to Ponder

Think about these questions, and take the time to write out your answers. Writing will help you think things through more thoroughly.

1. What is your reaction to hearing you've been tricked?

_____

_____

_____

_____

_____

Does it make you mad?

_____

2. **If it makes you mad, how are you likely to respond?**

_____

_____

_____

_____

_____

_____

Will that help or hurt your prospects for recovery?

_____

_____

_____

3. **Do you want to find another explanation, one that doesn't involve being tricked, because you don't like the idea of being tricked or "wrong"?**

_____

_____

_____

_____

4. **If you've been tricked, is that good or bad news for you?**

_____

_____

_____

4
....

How Panic Tricks You

To better understand the trick, I want you to think back to your first panic attack. I know you'll probably experience some unpleasant reactions to these memories, but do what you can to feel the fear and let it pass without getting into a struggle against it.

Think back to your first attack, the one you had even before you knew what a panic attack is. You got terribly afraid without knowing why. You might have just fled the situation without even thinking about why. But it's our nature to want explanations for what happens to us. If you're like most people, you tried to figure it out, either while you were still there, or after you fled the scene.

When you have a first panic attack and look around, you see no explanation in your immediate surroundings. If you had just had a close call with a runaway truck, or a wild animal, you would understand why you felt so afraid, and simply let it pass. But here, you don't see any explanation of your fear, any reason why you might feel so afraid.

If you're like most people, you want an explanation of your fear. You don't like to be afraid and have no explanation. So what do you do?

You guess. You make something up. And do you know what? People always make the same kind of guess: "I'm either dying, going crazy, fainting, losing control of myself, or all of the above." If you're like most people with panic, those are the feared outcomes you wrote about in Chapter 3.

That's the kind of guess people make, and they make it based on the symptoms they're feeling. It's a reasonable guess, under the circumstances. It certainly does seem as though something catastrophic is happening. But it's not. It tricked you, and you guessed wrong. A panic attack doesn't do any of those things.

But this is what most people guess when they have their first panic attack. People generally react by thinking that something is terribly wrong, either with their body or with their mind. Typical fears include dying, going crazy, fainting, or losing control of yourself in some terrible, permanent, and embarrassingly public way.

In this way, it tricks you into trying to protect yourself.

What about Fainting?

Fainting is one of the outcomes most feared during a panic attack, along with death and insanity. People frequently feel a peculiar lightheaded sensation during a panic attack, leading them to conclude they are about to faint. Even people who have never fainted in their life, and therefore don't know what if feels like to faint, are quick to guess that this feeling means they are about to faint.

It's a reasonable guess. It's just wrong. You're not about to faint. What this feeling does mean is that you're breathing poorly. Maybe you're hyperventilating, or maybe you're just breathing really short and shallow, from your chest. Either way, this kind of breathing leads you to exhale more carbon dioxide than you usually do. This produces a change in the pH of your blood, resulting in a slight reduction in the release of oxygen to your brain and causing an uncomfortable sensation of lightheadedness. You're getting plenty of oxygen to live on, and if you had to breathe like this the rest of your life, it wouldn't harm you.

Do you know what *does* cause a person to faint? Fainting is the result of a sudden big drop in your blood pressure. If your blood pressure drops to a significant degree, you might not get enough blood to your brain. Fainting is your body's way of protecting you from this. If you don't get enough blood to your brain, fainting brings your brain level down to the blood level.

What happens to your blood pressure during a panic attack? It goes up. Probably not a lot, but it does the *opposite* of what would cause you to faint. Fainting could only happen when some other physical circumstance or condition lowers your blood pressure so much that it overcomes this increase.

There are several conditions that can lead a person to faint even when their blood pressure is low. But if you're an adult with such a condition, you will already have a history of actual fainting episodes.

In the absence of these conditions, it would be *extremely* difficult to faint during a panic attack. So if you're a full-fledged adult with no history of fainting, you just don't have the physiology that would lead you to faint during a panic attack.

Fear and Danger

People tend to think that panic attacks mean there's something terribly wrong with them, physically or mentally. In fact, there's nothing wrong with your body, or your mind. Yes, there's a problem, for sure. You keep experiencing all these terrible fears and sensations when there seems to be no good reason for it. And you probably avoid lots of ordinary, valuable, or enjoyable activities for fear of having a panic attack. And you try to protect yourself in a variety of ways. Those are problems. But there's nothing wrong with your body or your mind. You're not ill or dying. You're not crazy, or even halfway there. You're just getting tricked, that's all.

Because of the trick, you experience real fear. It's in your breathing, in your muscles, in your heartbeat, in your production of adrenaline, in your digestive tract, and so on. It's real physical fear. You're not imagining it; it's an actual event. You've probably had people tell you "It's all in your head" in an effort to reassure you. They mean well, but it's not true. The fear is real. The problem is, you're experiencing this real fear when there's no real danger.

Most people tend to assume, without giving it much thought, "If I'm afraid, I must be in danger." Fear is often a useful signal. It warns us of danger, and mobilizes our resources to enable us to protect ourselves. But just as car alarms can go off in the absence of any thieves, it's quite common to feel afraid in the complete absence of any danger.

Can you think of any situations in which a person might be very afraid, even though they know beyond a shadow of a doubt, that they're not in any danger? Write your answer here:

_____

_____

_____

_____

People often answer this question with other people's fears. For instance, someone who's afraid of driving and malls, but doesn't mind heights in the least, will select "heights" as the answer. Someone who fears dogs but doesn't mind driving will tell me that "driving" is a situation in which people get afraid even though they know they're not in danger. This is because people always think somebody else's phobias are easier.

But what I'm asking about here is a situation in which you actually become afraid even though you know clearly that you're not in any danger. A person with a phobia, no matter how improbable, is never really sure they're not in danger, not in the moment of encountering the feared object or situation.

Try again . . .

_____

_____

_____

_____

You get extra points if you thought of a scary movie. The very existence of scary movies points to something very important about how our minds and bodies work. In our society, millions of people voluntarily turn out to attend a scary movie.

Manufactured Fear and Synthetic Danger

Look in the entertainment section of your local newspaper. Is there a scary movie playing at a theater near you? Not necessarily one of those slasher flicks full of blood, gore, and screaming teenage girls, but maybe a Stephen King–type horror show, a Hitchcock-style thriller, or something with regenerated dinosaurs and lost children; you're sure to find at least one film that's carefully calculated to scare the living daylights out of audiences.

You've read the ads and the reviews. You've talked to friends. You know the movie is supposed to be really scary, so you stand in line to buy tickets, hoping to get your money's worth. Maybe you buy some popcorn or nachos. Then you go inside and find good seats, with nobody blocking your view. The lights go down and commercials and previews start to run.

Then the scary movie begins. You tune out the red exit lights, the smell of popcorn, and the sound of somebody coughing two rows back. You watch the movie.

And you get scared. If the movie's as good as they say, you may get *very* scared—even though you know "it's only a movie." You hold your breath. You perch on the edge of your seat. Your body tenses up, you feel warm, your heart rate goes up. You may grip the arm of your seat (or your date) until your knuckles turn white, cover your eyes during the awful parts, or even find it necessary to leave. In short, your body responds as if the story were real, happening at that moment.

Of course, you're not really in any danger. Furthermore, you *know* you're not—but that doesn't matter. You experience a certain kind of physical discomfort in response to the film, and you react as if it were danger—a classic instance of the proverbial "fear of fear."

This is the artistry, the magic, of the scary movie. The film industry has people who are experts at getting you scared. They design sounds, images, plots, and characters to trick you into feeling fear, even though you're just sitting there eating your popcorn and feeling your shoes stick to the chewing gum on the floor. And strange as it may seem, millions of people pay cash to get scared witless. Others wait and rent the DVD, watch it in the comfort and convenience of their own homes—and still get scared.

This tells us something important about our species. We don't have to be in danger to get afraid. We can be in a situation where we know there's no danger at all, except maybe for the way the butter popcorn is affecting our cholesterol level. But we get afraid anyway. We don't have to be in real danger. All we need is to have some scary pictures and thoughts in our mind. Even though we know it's mere fiction, we still get afraid.

Do the people who get scared in the movie theater think that there's something wrong with them, or that their fear will have dire consequences? Of course not. Yet they're experiencing the same natural process you do when you have a panic attack. The only difference is that they paid for the privilege; you get it for free.

We have our own movie theater in the mind that can produce scary movies and, even more effectively than Hollywood, trick us into getting afraid.

Of course, the fact that the panic attack is undesired is the troublesome difference. Moviegoers willfully choose to go get scared, while your fear is an unwanted experience. Movie fear will pass in a few moments or hours, while the fear of someone with panic disorder can last a lifetime if he doesn't learn how to defuse it. But the trick is the same.

You experience discomfort, but respond as if it were danger.

Fight, Flight, and Freeze

It's very important to understand something about the physical symptoms you experience during a panic attack.

The physical symptoms of a panic attack are simply the product of your sympathetic nervous system. The sympathetic nervous system is the part of your central nervous system that is principally responsible for gearing you up to face a sudden danger, like a tiger or a prairie fire.

The symptoms of a panic attack are the same sophisticated, automatic physical responses that your body uses to alert you to danger and give you the physical energy to respond to it.

Our body is kind of an old model. When our bodies were "designed," the main danger we had to face was a big predator that saw us as a meal. And, even though our world has changed a lot since then, our bodies still respond to danger in the same way.

They respond in three ways, actually. When our bodies get a "danger" signal, they respond by preparing us for either *fight*, *flight*, or their less well-known cousin, *freeze*. Which one? It depends on the circumstances. If my attacker looks smaller or weaker than me, then it's probably a good idea to fight. If the enemy is bigger and stronger, but slower, I'm going to choose flight, and run away. And if I'm up against a predator that looks both stronger and faster than me, then I'll probably stand real still, and hold my breath in the hope it doesn't see (or smell) so well—that's freeze.

If you think carefully about the physical symptoms you experience during a panic attack, you can probably see that most of them have some adaptive value in a dangerous situation. They would all serve, one way or another, to help you survive an encounter with a predator.

Imagine for a minute that you're a prehistoric cave dweller, sitting by your campfire, roasting a mastodon steak for dinner, when suddenly a 900-pound saber-toothed tiger appears, its eyes gleaming fiendishly in the firelight. In an instant, you weigh your options. Can you grab a burning branch from the fire and brandish it as you charge toward the beast, hoping it will turn tail and run? Or what if *you* turn and run, hoping to reach the nearby river and swim to safety before the big cat catches you? Or is it possible that you can escape the tiger's notice by standing stock-still, hoping that it will be content to snatch your steak and wander away to eat it in peace?

As these thoughts race through your mind, several things take place within your body. Your heart rate increases, and your breath becomes short and shallow like a sprinter's. Your muscles need that oxygen, either to charge or to run. An adrenaline rush supercharges your body with the extra energy you need to fight or run away. You feel cramping and discomfort in your digestive tract as your body makes some rapid shifts in your blood flow, redirecting blood away from your stomach to more vital parts of your body, such as your brain and heart. There's not much point in using energy to digest your own food right now; better to save it for fight or flight, and do your digesting later. You break out in a sweat, which cools your body to counteract the heat you generate as your body produces its emergency supply of energy. The sweat also makes you slippery and harder for the tiger to grab ahold of.

All these symptoms are rapid, sophisticated responses developed by humans over many thousands of centuries to maximize your chances of survival in a dangerous world. What a finely tuned mechanism your body is. In an instant it can produce such radical changes to protect you from a predator.

There's just one problem.

You're in the canned juice aisle, or in a staff meeting, or in expressway traffic. There is no saber-toothed tiger. Yet your body hasn't lost its ability to respond to this kind of life-threatening emergency, and it can get tricked into reacting this way at the most inappropriate times.

This is very much like the problem some people have with their dogs. It's good to have a dog that barks when strangers approach your house. But it's a problem if the dog also barks at the kids next door. The dog needs to be trained so it can tell the difference between kids and burglars. If you have panic attacks, you need training too.

The watchdog sees kids playing and mistakes them for burglars. You experience discomfort and mistake it for danger. The watchdog needs training so it can

> ## Adrenaline Heroes
>
> Have you ever watched or heard an interview with someone who performed a heroic act, like pulling someone from a burning building or a train track? They always say the same thing—that they weren't feeling particularly afraid or brave—they just did what they had to do.
>
> They had all that energy pumping—the adrenaline, the change in blood flow, the change in breathing—but they used it, and so they didn't particularly notice its effects. They were too busy dealing with the emergency.
>
> If they were to experience that energy in a different situation, something without an obvious emergency, like a crowded supermarket or a long wait in a waiting room, it would be another matter entirely.

notice some of the key characteristics of children (short, high-pitched voices, big eyes, lack of guns and pry bars) that distinguish them from burglars. You need training so you can better distinguish discomfort from danger.

The Trickiest Part of the Trick

Here's the sneakiest part of the trick, the part that gets people feeling like a bug in a spider web. The responses that help you with danger are pretty much the exact opposite of the ones that help with discomfort.

If the problem you face is danger, you need to protect yourself, and you can do that with fight, flight, or freeze. But if the problem you face is discomfort, the last thing you need is to get worked up about it. That just makes you more uncomfortable. What works with discomfort is to calm down, to "chill out," to take a passive attitude and give the situation time to improve on its own. The late Claire Weekes, an Australian physician and author who became famous for her work with panic and anxiety, described this as "floating" through the panic.

So when your body responds to the wrong signal, when you get tricked into treating panic as if it were dangerous, you end up doing all the things that will make the attack last longer and be more severe. As your body automatically gears up to face a nonexistent danger, your best efforts go toward making you feel worse.

Think about how you handle a headache. Ideally, you accept the fact that you have a headache, and you do what you can to relax and allow it to pass as quickly as possible. It probably wouldn't occur to you to get angry at the headache, or at yourself for having one. You certainly wouldn't yell at yourself or bang your head against the wall in an effort to rid yourself of the headache.

Relax or I'll Shoot

This isn't a true story, it's made up. It's not even my original story. I based it on an idea originally published in *Acceptance and Commitment Therapy*, by Steven Hayes, Kirk Strosahl, and Kelly Wilson.

A man comes into my office, a man I know to be someone who says exactly what he means, and who does exactly what he says. He has a gun, and he points it at me. He says, "Dave, I want you to move all the furniture from this office out into the waiting room, or else I'm going to shoot you."

What do I do?

I move the furniture into the waiting room, and I live.

A week goes by, and the man returns to my office a second time, with the same gun. He points it at me and says, "Dave, I want you to sing the 'Star-Spangled Banner'—first verse will be sufficient—or else I'm going to shoot you."

What's the outcome?

I sing the "Star-Spangled Banner," and all is well (except for those who had to hear me sing it).

A week later, the man comes back a third time, with the same gun. This time, he has an associate with him.

The associate wheels in a cart with an electronic device. The man says, "Dave, this is a state-of-the-art lie detector. It's infallible. It can detect any emotion you experience."

"My associate is going to hook you up to the equipment. I'm gonna hold my gun on you. Then I want you to relax. Or else I'm going to shoot you."

What happens?

Big trouble. I'm a goner.

Why is this so? Why can I succeed in moving the furniture, and singing the song, and yet fail so miserably at calming myself? The reason is simple to state. The rule that governs the "real world" is different from the rule that governs my internal world of thoughts, physical sensations, and emotions.

The rule that governs the "real world" is this: the harder I try, and the more I struggle against something, the more likely I am to get what I want. If I set my sight on a goal and persevere, I will probably get it, so long as I keep working at it.

The rule that governs my internal world is quite different: the harder I try, and the more I struggle against something, the more likely I am to get what I don't want.

That's why it's so clear, in the example above, that neither I, nor most mortals, could relax under those circumstances. The more I struggle against my fear, the more afraid I become.

When You Fall for the Trick

You wake up to a sunny day and feel pretty good, so you decide to try going to a grocery store you usually avoid. You kill time until 10:45, when you hope traffic will be light and the store uncrowded. While you're waiting to leave, you wonder if you should wait for an even better day but decide you'll be okay as long as you bring your water bottle and cellular phone.

As you drive to the store, you picture it being crowded. You try to block that image, but it persists, and you grasp the steering wheel harder in response. You remember the last panic attack you had and say a little prayer that you won't have trouble today. You hope the prayer helps. You find yourself worrying about a nervous breakdown as you wait at a red light, so you try to distract yourself by singing a song and slapping your thigh in time to the music. Still, you can't help but wonder if this is a bad idea. You decide you'll just step into the store and see how you feel. If you feel too anxious, you'll pretend you just remembered an appointment (in case anyone is watching you) and leave.

At the parking lot, the row closest to the store is full, but you see a woman wheeling her cart toward a car there. You decide to wait for that space instead of parking two rows back, in case you panic and want to rush home. Clenching your teeth and tensing your shoulders, you wait impatiently as she slowly loads her car. She glances at you as she closes the trunk, and you wonder if she thinks you're doing something odd. "I could have parked and been in the store already," you think irritably.

You feel sweaty and lightheaded as you enter the store. You remember that you should take a deep breath, but when you take a big gulp of air you feel even worse than before, as if you can't get enough air, and your chest starts to hurt. You think maybe you'll just pick up an item or two from the front display and quickly leave. Or maybe you should leave right away.

As you hesitate, a clerk offers you a free newspaper and asks if you'd like a trial subscription. You don't want the newspaper, but you don't want to hurt his feelings, so you try to hide your mounting anxiety as he drones on about the offer. Fearing that you're about to pass out, you look around for a wall or a cart to lean on but see nothing within your reach. You don't want to reveal your anxiety by walking over to the wall, so you tighten all your muscles and ask God to keep you erect. Your heart is pounding so loudly that it takes a few moments for you to notice that the clerk has stopped talking. As soon as you do, you hastily fill out the subscription form for the newspaper you don't want, then quickly flee the store, mumbling something about an appointment. Once outside, you heave a sigh of relief and vow never to return to that store again.

5

....

What Keeps Panic in Your Life

Why do people continue to be fooled by the panic trick? Why don't they see through the trick after the first dozen attacks, or even the first hundred? Why doesn't their repeated failure to die, go crazy, or lose control lead them to realize that these "attacks," scary as they seem, are simply not dangerous?

Two main factors stop people from outgrowing the panic in a natural, spontaneous way. One is that, ironically, the very things people do in an effort to help themselves actually have the opposite effect, blocking their progress and getting them further "stuck."

This represents the core of the panic trick. Panic actually tricks you into acting in ways that maintain and strengthen the panic and phobias. It doesn't just fool you once. It doesn't just fool you 100 times, or 1000. It fools you into building panic and phobias into your life, every day. This, more than anything, is why people find that, "the harder I try, the worse I get," because they're trying things that make the problem worse, rather than better.

They're trying the proverbial "putting out a fire with gasoline." The first step in putting out a fire, if you're been pouring gasoline on it, is to notice that you're using gasoline rather than water. The second step is to stop using the gasoline. It's the same with panic and phobias. Even if you don't know what else to do about

Reader Advisory

Prepare yourself for some surprise as you read about these self-protective methods. When I describe some responses that usually make your situation worse, I'm going to include some things that you probably thought were helpful. When I identify the bad guys in this plot, I'm going to include some that you probably thought were good guys.

the fire, it will be a good step to stop pouring gasoline on it. Once you stop doing that, you can figure out something else, something better, to do.

People make their phobias worse by trying to protect themselves by various strategies including:

- Avoidance
- Protective rules & rituals
- Superstitions
- Support people and support objects
- Distraction
- Fighting the fear.

What do you do to try to prevent panic attacks?

_____

_____

_____

_____

_____

_____

_____

_____

The other factor that makes phobias worse, as we shall see, isn't a choice you make. It's an involuntary, or automatic, way of thinking that you have to learn to manage. It's anticipatory worry.

Avoidance

Avoidance, of feared places, objects, and activities, is the hallmark of a phobia. Phobias prevent people from participating in countless ordinary activities that most other people take for granted. This includes such activities as:

- driving freely to visit friends, or to go shopping
- taking your children to the zoo or other crowded recreational site
- flying to a desirable vacation spot, or to visit loved ones who live far away
- meeting a friend for lunch at a crowded café
- joining a club, or signing up for a class
- describing a project at a staff meeting
- going to a party

- going to the doctor, or the dentist
- shopping in a large, crowded store
- and almost any other kind of ordinary activity you can think of.

What places, objects, and activities do you avoid?

_____

_____

_____

_____

_____

_____

_____

It's important to see that avoidance isn't just the result of a phobia. It's also how the phobia continues to reinvent and maintain itself in your life. Phobias perpetuate themselves by keeping you *away* from the things you fear. This:

- prevents you from discovering anything new about your fear that might help resolve it
- keeps you believing that disaster would strike if you stopped "protecting" yourself
- leads you to try harder to "make sure" you're safe, in ways that make you more anxious.

When you avoid the thing you fear, you don't actually get to find out what would have happened if you had encountered it. You're just left with a feeling of relief that you "dodged a bullet," and your scary ideas about what a "near miss" you had. You think you just barely managed to protect yourself, and you only hope that you'll be able to continue to keep yourself "safe" in the future.

The sense of relief you get when you avoid or retreat from a feared situation, feels welcome. But it also makes you more anxious about the future and more likely to avoid it again. You're getting a small amount of immediate relief, but you're going to pay for it.

Protective Rules and Rituals

People also develop interesting ways of doing things that they hope will keep them safe and ward off panic. These usually involve some element of partial avoidance, and offer a way for that person to go into a feared situation and still feel "protected" because they're avoiding some key element they fear. These rules all have some kernel of logic behind them, in the sense that following the rules might buy you a little temporary comfort. But when you come to believe that your safety, sanity, and survival depend upon your adherence to these rules, this makes you a candidate for panic disorder.

Here are some of the rules and rituals others have used:

A classic case I've heard described was of a man who was afraid he would panic if he went out for a walk and then saw how far he had to walk to get home. He tried to resolve this problem by walking backward on the return trip so that he wouldn't see how far he had to go.

- limit their shopping to off peak times, when the store will be less crowded
- buy fewer than ten items, so they can always go through the express line
- only shop in areas of the grocery store from which they can see the exit
- avoid intersections from which they have to make a left turn
- stay in the right-hand lane while driving on a divided highway
- always take an aisle seat, so they won't be "trapped" in the middle.

What protective rules and rituals do you use?

_____

_____

_____

_____

_____

_____

Superstitions

Superstitions are beliefs people recognize aren't really true but feel compelled to follow anyway in the spirit of "it can't hurt!" or "better safe than sorry." A superstitious ritual that's commonplace in many homes is the old "knock on wood" routine. "Lucky objects" like a rabbit's foot or a lucky sweater are also widely used.

For instance, a common superstition is the idea that the particular clothes a person wore on the day of a severe panic attack somehow have special significance. People will often avoid wearing certain combinations of clothes because they once wore that particular shirt and pants on the day of a particularly bad panic attack. Thereafter, they only wear those items as parts of different ensembles. Unfortunately, when you adhere to superstitious rituals in the belief that

That Tricky Wizard

Remember the scene in *The Wizard of Oz* when Dorothy looks behind the curtain and sees that the seemingly all-powerful wizard is actually a short little nerdy guy? "Pay no attention to that man behind the curtain!" he desperately commands her, because when she realizes that the Wizard is just that little guy behind the curtain, she'll lose her fear of him. That's what your phobia tells you, too. If it can prevent you from looking behind the curtain, it can keep you chronically afraid.

To persist, the phobia has to trick you. Break the trick, systematically and persistently, and you break the phobia.

they protect you from panic, you end up reinforcing your sense of vulnerability, and this works to strengthen and maintain the problem.

If you go to the 12th floor of a high-rise building and then go up one more flight, you come to the 13th floor. But many buildings call it the 14th. The superstition about the number 13 is so mainstream that building owners have to take it into account. If you have superstitious beliefs, you have a lot of company.

Do you have any superstitions? What are they?

_____

_____

_____

_____

_____

_____

_____

_____

Support People and Support Objects

Another way that people try to protect themselves is by reliance on a "support person," or a "support object."

People who limit their travel to a particular "safe zone" can often go outside of that zone without panicking if they are accompanied by a "support person"—someone in whom they place a lot of trust, who knows them well, who will comfort and help them if they have a panic attack. Because they feel protected, people usually don't panic in the presence of their support person.

Do you have a support person, or people? List them here.

_____   _____

_____   _____

_____   _____

_____   _____

A support object is an object people carry with them because they believe it will help them avoid a panic attack, or help protect them if they do have one. Common support objects include water bottles, cellular phones, favorite snack foods, and photos of loved ones, but there are a million variations on this theme. I've had clients who kept running shoes in their car (in case they had to run away); kept buckets in their car (in case they had to vomit, urinate, or have a bowel movement while "trapped" in the car); and carried my business card at all times (if they ended up in the psychiatric ward, the doctors there would know to call me).

Do you remember Dumbo's feather? Dumbo was an elephant who could fly— as long as he held his magic feather securely in his trunk. One day he dropped the feather and, after an initial moment of panic, learned he could fly just fine without it. Dumbo's feather was a support object.

Do you have any support objects? What are they?

_____   _____

_____   _____

_____   _____

_____   _____

At first, people often say they have no support objects, but when they take a moment or two to reflect on it, realize that they do have some. Maybe that's true for you. Relying on support objects becomes such an automatic habit that it's easy to overlook.

Distraction

Distraction is another common way that people try to protect themselves. They've realized that when their attention is fully engaged with some task or subject, and they're not thinking about their fear problem, they're much less likely to panic. So they try to deliberately distract themselves from anything related to the subject of their fears. The problem is, this strategy leads them to believe that they are so vulnerable that all they have to do is think the "wrong" thing, and panic will sweep them away.

Naturally, this makes a person more fearful over time.

There are countless creative ways that people distract themselves. They sing or hum to themselves; add random numbers; balance their checkbook; play the license plate game of watching for license plates from other states; count cars, trees, or whatever objects happen to be at hand, and so on.

What are some of the ways you distract yourself?

_____

_____

_____

_____

_____

_____

_____

_____

Fighting the Fear

When people become afraid, they instinctively try to fight and resist the fear. Sometimes they treat the fear as if it were an external force, like a strong wind that threatens to knock them over. They stiffen their body, tighten up their muscles, and hold their breath. These efforts, unfortunately, make them more anxious rather than less.

Sometimes they resist their fearful thoughts. They argue with the thoughts, and the thoughts appear to argue back, and this produces the same result that comes from tensing their body. They feel more upset, rather than less.

Sometimes people fight the fear by making a direct appeal to God. A simple prayer that asks God to guide, comfort, and strengthen you through adversity is fine when it's consistent with your spiritual beliefs. But all too often, people with panic and phobias pray in a way that might better be considered "nagging God." Like this:

> Dear God, as I drive to Aunt Ruth's today, please keep the temperature in the moderate range, no more than 70 degrees, because I had that big panic attack when it was so hot last summer. Please keep the roads pretty empty, I don't want to get stuck in a traffic

jam. Please have all the green lights ready, especially that left turn lane onto Grand Avenue. And, God, please, no fire trucks this time, okay? Please keep my pulse an even 70 beats per minute, let my breathing be smooth and regular, and my head clear. And God, I don't want to be thinking about my breathing today, okay? God? Are you listening? I said I don't want to be thinking about my breathing today, and already I'm thinking about it. God, are you riding with me today or what?

Do you try to fight the fear? In what specific ways?

_____

_____

_____

_____

_____

So there are a variety of ways, beyond plain avoidance, in which people seek to protect themselves from panic when they venture into feared territory or activities. At this point, you might be thinking "Hey, wait a minute! I do those things. They're good things, they help me go further, and do more, than I'm usually able to do."

And well they might. Sometimes, the use of such devices is the only way a person can get started on the road to recovery. They can be a good thing, if they get you started when you would otherwise continue to rely on avoidance.

But it's important to notice that, while they can help you get started, they also tend to maintain the panic over time. When you rely on these self-protective devices, you are being deprived of the opportunity to find out that you survive intact without them. You will continue to believe that they save you from danger, and that you need them. This is how panic tricks you into continuing to feel afraid.

That's how it is with these protective methods. If you can use them briefly to get you started, and then discard them, more power to you. But as soon as you become reliant on them, they become part of the problem and lead you to look for more and more reassurance.

> *It's like that old vaudeville joke. Two guys are having a conversation. Periodically, the first guy interrupts the other to make an unusual croaking sound. Finally, the second man asks, "Why do you keep making that sound?"*
>
> *"It keeps the elephants away."*
>
> *"Don't be ridiculous! There isn't an elephant within 1000 miles!"*
>
> *"See? It works!"*

For instance, if you fear driving, you might be comforted by carrying a cellular phone. As time goes by, you might feel the need to have it ready for action on the seat next to you. Then it seems like a good idea to have a speed call all lined up and ready to go with the push of a single button. You might decide to confirm that a particular person is available to take your call, "just in case." A backup person will seem like a good idea at some point. An extra battery for your phone can't hurt, either. And so it goes.

Like Dumbo, you'll continue to believe that you need your magic feather. Like the vaudeville guys, you'll continue to believe that "it works!" This solidifies your suspicion that you're vulnerable and need protection from panic.

A Case of Spousal Support

A woman came to one of my support groups for the first time with her husband. She introduced herself and explained that she was afraid to drive at night, because she believed she would faint if she had to drive in the dark.

I asked her if it would be okay to discuss this and she agreed. It seemed to me like a good chance to help the group work with a new example of how the fear worked, and also to help the newcomer get off to a good start.

ME: Where do you work?

HER: I work the night shift at a factory.

ME: Oh? You have a night job?

HER: Yes, that's right. My husband works nights, too. It's not so bad, working nights, since we're on similar schedules.

ME: How long have you held this job?

HER: It will be seven years in May.

ME: Is it full time?

HER: No, I work three nights a week.

ME: How do you get to work?

HER: I drive.

ME: You drive to your night job?

HER: Yes.

ME: Hmm, I'm surprised to hear that. How many times have you fainted while driving to your night job?

HER: None.

ME: You've never fainted while driving to or from your night job?

Use these self-protective methods, if you have no other way to get started, but be wary of relying on them for significant amounts of time.

If you're like most people, you might feel a little embarrassed to admit to some of these methods. But that's okay, nobody ever died of embarrassment. It's very helpful to take an inventory of these methods because they probably contribute to keeping you stuck, rather than helping you recover.

It's best to let them go—one at a time, when *you* decide to let them go. To help you prepare for this step, periodically return to your lists of protections that you started in this chapter, and add to them as you remember and notice other protective devices and rules.

HER: No.

ME: Okay. You've come here because you're afraid of driving at night, just the thought of it can make you panic. It was dark when you came here tonight, yes?

HER: Yes.

ME: And you didn't faint. Okay. Let's see. Almost seven years, let's say 50 weeks a year, 3 nights a week, so you've driven to this night job at least a thousand times, probably more?

HER: Yes, that's about right.

ME: So, you've driven to your night job more than a thousand times in the last seven years, is that right? Without ever fainting?

HER: Correct.

ME: Well, Ma'am, I couldn't help but notice, that you think you'll faint if you drive in the dark, but you've done it more than a thousand times without fainting. How do you explain your failure to faint?

HER: My husband, Horace, he follows me in his car.

It made perfect sense to her that somehow having her husband drive behind her was preventing her from fainting. It was as if he was driving a late model Plasmamobile back there, keeping her blood pressure up above the level that would have produced fainting.

Of course, he wasn't really preventing her from fainting, but she couldn't come to that conclusion as long as she relied on him to follow her. As long as she relied on this "support person," she had no evidence that she could cope without him. And so she continued to believe that she was vulnerable to fainting at night, even though it had never happened to her. She subsequently let him fall further and further behind, and eventually stopped having him follow her. She was then able to see and believe that she could drive alone, at night, without fainting.

Looking back at your answers to the previous exercises in this chapter, summarize the self-protective methods you have used in attempting to prevent panic attacks. List them here:

_____

_____

_____

_____

_____

_____

_____

_____

_____

_____

For each self-protective method on the above list, what would happen if you simply let it go?

_____

_____

_____

_____

_____

_____

_____

_____

_____

_____

How to Defuse the Trick

The ultimate goal of recovery from these problems is to be able to live freely *and* feel good. But when a person has chronic panic attacks, it often seems as though they have to choose between comfort and freedom. If they go outside their comfort zone, or violate any of their self protective rules, they may panic. If they obey all the self-protective rules in order to feel "safe," they feel imprisoned, and miss out on a lot of life.

A person with chronic panic attacks has generally fallen into the habit of putting comfort first. They make decisions based on what will help them feel comfortable, or at least not panic, rather than on what will allow them to live freely, go where they want, and do what they want.

There's a reason for this.

If you start to panic in a grocery store, you can probably bring that panic attack to a quick end simply by going out to your car. As soon as those electronic doors start to open, you start to feel better. If you retreat, or protect yourself, you can feel better almost immediately.

On the other hand, if you stay in the situation and work with the panic, rather than retreat or protect yourself, you will advance your recovery. You won't "fix" the entire problem that day, and you will temporarily feel worse than if you ran out to the parking lot, but it's a step in the direction that will ultimately lead you to recovery.

Quite naturally, people tend to respond to panic based on what helps them feel better *right away*. They choose immediate comfort rather than long-term freedom, perhaps thinking they will deal with becoming free tomorrow. But tomorrow never comes. You pay for immediate relief by making yourself more sensitive to the fear and creating a worse problem in the long run. You get fooled into thinking that you are far more vulnerable than you really are. It's not a good trade.

Don't make yourself more comfortable in the present by contributing to a phobia in the future. The "Golden Rule" of recovery is: *Choose long-term freedom, not immediate comfort.*

You can rely on this guideline to help you make the countless choices you will confront in your self-help work. So long as you regularly make choices that promote your long-term freedom, rather than your immediate comfort, you can feel satisfied that you are on the right path. That doesn't mean it will be easy, or comfortable, but you'll know you're headed in the right direction.

Imagine a situation in which you have experienced a panic attack in the past. It may be one that you've described in a previous exercise. Write the situation here.

_____

_____

_____

_____

_____

_____

What could you do in this situation that would give the most immediate relief?

_____

_____

_____

_____

_____

What could you do in this situation that would give you the most long-term freedom from fear?

_____

_____

_____

_____

_____

If this situation occurred today, which course of action would you choose—and why? (Be honest.)

_____

_____

_____

_____

_____

Anticipatory Worry

The second factor, **anticipation**, is the sparkplug of panic, the source of the intermittent energy that keeps the whole process moving along in a circular fashion. It consists of thoughts that suggest terrible things are going to happen to you.

Representative examples would include the following:

- What if I freak out and drive off the bridge?
- What if I try to breathe, and nothing happens?
- What if I blush bright red when I go to write a check, and they think I'm a criminal?
- What if I start panicking when I'm stuck in line at the grocery store?

Most anticipation takes the form of "what if" thinking, although it sometimes takes other, more subtle forms, such as:

- I've been doing pretty well with my panic recovery, so far.
- I hope I don't panic when I give my presentation Friday.
- Hey, I haven't had a panic attack all week.

Anticipation doesn't always have to be a verbal thought that can be expressed in a sentence. It can also take the form of images that suddenly occur to you, such as an image of you having a panic attack at a particular place or time, or an anxious sensation that occurs to you as you think about a future event.

What "what if" thoughts do you experience when you anticipate that you may have a panic attack?

_____

_____

_____

_____

Now look away from this list and _try not to think these thoughts_ for thirty seconds. Does it work?

_____

I didn't think so.

Anticipation is essentially automatic and involuntary, meaning that there aren't any good ways by which you can simply tell yourself to "stop thinking about that" and make it work. Instead, this usually has the same effect as the effort to ban books. "Banned in Boston" used to be an advertising slogan because people are naturally more interested in books that are banned. In the same way, telling yourself to "stop thinking about it" normally leads you to think about it more.

Much anticipation is subliminal, meaning that you don't quite notice on a conscious level what you're thinking. But the thoughts still influence you. And when you do notice specific thoughts, you're likely to get embroiled in an argument with those thoughts, which serves to increase your level of anxiety.

So there are two main ways these anticipatory thoughts cause you trouble. In the first case, they cause you trouble when they exist in the background, as subliminal sources of influence, and you don't even notice their presence. They influence your mood without your noticing, or having a chance to do anything about it.

In the second case, they cause you trouble when they come to your immediate attention and get you embroiled in a struggle to "stop thinking about it." Fighting your thoughts in such a way will almost always make them more persistent, and you more anxious.

What you need to cope with these thoughts is a method that enables you to notice and accept the thoughts without fighting and arguing with them. In Chapter 19, I'll suggest some ways you can do this.

6
....

Dissecting a Panic Attack

One of the things you're up against with panic is that the experience of an attack seems so overwhelming. It's very hard to make sense of what's happening. Even the next day, after it's over, you may find it hard to describe or explain what happened to make you so afraid. So it will be very helpful if you can become more aware of what is happening and be able to divide the attack into its component parts.

A panic attack can seem like such a singular, overwhelming experience that people often don't recognize that it consists of four different kinds of symptoms. It's very helpful to know this, because the symptoms don't all work the same, and the different kinds of symptoms usually require different kinds of reactions in order to calm yourself.

Let's do something now to help you feel less overwhelmed next time. Let's break your typical panic attack into its four component parts.

The ability to break a panic attack into its different parts *as you experience it* will become an important tool in your recovery. It will give you several advantages, including:

1. You will better understand what you're up against when you experience a panic attack, and will feel less confused and overwhelmed.

2. You will be better prepared to respond to the different parts of an attack in ways that effectively calm you, rather than further agitate you.

3. You will come to see that what we call a "panic attack" is not an attack at all, but a *reaction*. This will make it much easier for you to take on the accepting attitude that you need to calm yourself.

4. Familiarity with the parts of an attack will help you to better observe what is going on during a panic attack. When you assume the role of *observer*, this helps to give you a little emotional distance from the turmoil of the attack. Simply speaking, when you experience a panic attack, you're either going to assume the role of an observer or a victim. The observer's better.

The four different kinds of symptoms are these:
1. Physical sensations
2. Thoughts
3. Emotions
4. Behaviors

Physical sensations are probably the part of the panic attack that gets most of your attention. There are many physical sensations that people experience as part of a panic attack. Think about your first full-blown panic attack, or another major one you recall clearly, and **list the physical symptoms you experienced.**

_____ _____

_____ _____

_____ _____

_____ _____

_____ _____

Thoughts are an important part of a panic attack, and are almost always misunderstood by the person experiencing an attack. **What thoughts do you typically experience during a panic attack? Include all the thoughts, especially the ones that sound terribly extreme and unrealistic now.**

_____

_____

_____

_____

_____

An *emotion* is a "gut reaction," an overall feeling about a particular event or situation. Emotions are feelings such as glad, sad, mad, afraid, jealous, and so on.

Emotions are difficult for many people to put into words. Let's give it a try right now. **What emotions do you typically experience during a panic attack?**

_____ _____

_____ _____

_____ _____

_____ _____

_____ _____

Behaviors differ from physical sensations, thoughts, and emotions in that they are what you do, rather than what you feel or think. They may be as subtle as eye movements or as obvious as bolting for the door. **What behaviors do you engage in during a panic attack?**

_____

_____

_____

_____

_____

_____

_____

Notice Your Behaviors

When I ask people who are afflicted with panic attacks to tell me what the four categories of symptoms are, they generally get the first three but virtually never mention the category of behaviors. People feel so assaulted and victimized by the attack, they don't even notice that they're *doing* things that are part of the attack—like holding their breath. But they feel the uncomfortable effects of it, and this makes the panic worse. So it will be very helpful for you to become aware of what you actually do during a panic attack—your behaviors.

The most obvious of the classic behaviors in a panic attack is flight. People often flee the scene. But before they do, they engage in other behaviors. Here are some common ones. People experiencing a panic attack often:

- Hold their breath
- Tense the muscles of their neck, shoulders, jaw, and other parts of the body

- Lean against a wall for "support"
- Withdraw into themselves, and become less involved in what goes on around them
- Try to act in ways so that no one notices that they're nervous
- Prepare for escape, by moving to the door, keeping their coat on, etc.

What panic behaviors have in common is that they're all responses to the panic trick. People experience discomfort, and respond as if it were danger. When you respond this way, you're literally getting tricked into behaving in ways that will make the problem worse.

Fleeing makes the problem worse because it reinforces the mistaken idea that you just barely escaped a terrible calamity, and it suggests that your luck may be running out. Holding your breath, and tensing your body, makes you more uncomfortable, and produces additional symptoms. Withdrawing into yourself will lead you to become more focused on your discomfort, and make it seem worse. And the other behaviors I listed above all involve some way of resisting the present experience and trying to fight the anxiety. This almost always makes a person feel worse, and gets them thinking they're really in a struggle for survival.

Think about Your Thoughts

One big problem people have with their thoughts is that in the moment of a panic attack, they fail to recognize that this symptom is just that—a symptom. It's not a sixth sense that gives you advance warning of something that's about to happen. It's not a warning from your guardian angel. It's just a way of being anxious. The real message of the scary thought during a panic attack is not the literal meaning of the words in the thought. The thought, like all panic and anxiety symptoms, has to be interpreted.

The problem people have is that they automatically assume the thought is literally true, and their body responds as if it were true.

Consider this. If you sat talking with someone who kept jiggling his leg during the conversation, you would probably make some interpretation of what that jiggling meant. You probably wouldn't take it literally, and think it meant he wanted to play football, or go jogging. You would probably interpret it as a sign of nervousness. In the same way, if he bit his fingernails, you wouldn't take it literally and think he was hungry, or wanted to eat himself up. You'd probably interpret it as a sign of nervousness.

When you have these scary thoughts of death, insanity, and loss of control during a panic attack, these are also symptoms that need to be interpreted. They're not about death and insanity any more than the leg-jiggling is about football, or the nail-biting about hunger or cannibalism.

These thoughts mean you're nervous. Nothing more, nothing less. They mean the same thing as the dry mouth, the labored breathing, and the racing heart. You're nervous. Or afraid, or anxious, or scared, or whatever word you want to use.

It's usually hard to see the extent to which your thoughts were exaggerated and untrue until *after* the panic attack is over. The trick is to get a different perspective on your thoughts *while* the attack is still going on. Developing the habit of noticing your thoughts, and making an interpretation of what they mean, rather than just taking them at face value, will be a big step in this direction.

It's a little harder to acquire the habit of making an interpretation of thoughts than it is with the physical symptoms. When you're afraid, your first instinct is likely going to be to take those thoughts literally, rather than stopping to interpret them. But this is a habit that you can develop with practice. The use of a panic diary, which I describe in Chapter 16, will help you develop this new habit.

Thoughts versus Emotions

People often confuse thoughts with emotions, so let's take a moment to distinguish between them. A thought is our attempt to interpret a particular event, to give it a meaning. For instance, I might see a traffic light turning yellow and think it's a signal to stop. Someone else might see the same light and think it means they need to speed up and get through it before it turns red. I might see someone frown and think they're mad at me. Someone else might think that person is worried, not mad. Thoughts are our interpretations of what we observe in the world, and in ourselves.

Our thoughts can be true or false, and are often mixtures of both. They are guesses about reality. If I measure someone's height with a tape measure, and I do it correctly, I have a true description of that person's height. If I just glance at that person and estimate his height, I probably won't get his height exactly right. And, my thought of how tall he is will likely be influenced by other factors that don't have anything to do with his height. Similarly, if somebody scares me while I'm walking down a dark street and I run away, I will probably remember him as larger than he really was. My thoughts can be influenced by a lot of factors, particularly my emotional state at the time.

Thoughts and emotions are connected, but they're not the same. Emotions don't try to describe the real world, so they can't be shown to be either true or false. They're simply our reactions to what we think is the real world. Since they're internal reactions, rather than descriptions of the world, there's no "true or false" aspect to them. There's nothing to test, no proof to obtain. Emotions need to be accepted, rather than tested or evaluated. When we resist our feelings, we're essentially fighting or arguing with ourselves. That makes us feel more anxious. That's not what you want to do during a panic attack.

People often blend these two different symptoms—thoughts and emotions—together as one. They'll say things like "I feel like I'm going to die." This blends the different kinds of symptoms together in ways that make it hard for you to respond. "I'm going to die" isn't a feeling, it's a thought. It might be true or false. What's usually happening here is that a person:

(a) observes physical sensations: "I'm dizzy and hot. My left arm is tingly."

(b) has an automatic thought (makes an interpretation) about what those sensations mean: "What if I have a heart attack right here? I could die!"

(c) has an emotional reaction to the thought of dying; feels afraid.

This kind of blending makes it much harder to soothe yourself. For instance, there isn't much I can do to help myself calm down from the feeling that I'm going to die. I can argue with it and tell myself I'm not going to die, but arguing with myself and my emotions will most likely just get me more upset. I can run and find help, but since I'm not really dying, there isn't much the emergency room staff can do to help me, because they'll see I'm not dying. Only when I break the attack into its component parts can I start responding to the thoughts, physical sensations, and emotions in ways that will help me calm down.

Separating Thoughts from Emotions

Let's replay the "I'm going to die" scenario the way you might once you've become pretty good at noticing the different parts of an attack and making appropriate interpretations and responses. It might go something like this:

(a) observes physical sensations: "I'm dizzy and hot. My left arm is tingly."

(b) has an automatic thought (makes an interpretation) about what those sensations mean: "What if I have a heart attack right here? I could die!"

(c) has an emotional reaction to the thought of dying; feels afraid.

(d) has a thought about what the thought of dying means: "oh crap, I'm starting to panic. Damn! What is wrong with me? When am I gonna stop doing this? I probably will give myself a heart attack if I keep this up!"

(e) has emotional reactions to the thought of panic: anger, shame, and disgust.

(f) changes thoughts to a more accepting tone: "Why do I...oh all right, let's just take care of business here. This stinks, but I'm not gonna beat up on myself. I've been through this before. I guess I better start going through my panic steps."

(g) takes action: begins belly breathing.

(h) observes reduction in physical sensations: "I'm not so dizzy, and my arm feels better."

(i) has thought about the change: "OK, that's better."

(j) has emotional reaction to the change: feels less afraid.

If you're having a lot of trouble with panic attacks, this example may seem unrealistic, or out of reach for you. That's okay. The rest of this book can help you get there. For now, it's enough to see how realizing that the thoughts mean fear, rather than danger, can give you an opportunity to change what happens next.

Responding as described above is really a matter of habit, and you can probably acquire the habit. The best way to acquire the habit is this:

Practice, practice, practice.

Over time, with repetition, these new ways of responding to the panic symptoms will become more automatic. Is this easy? Not at all. I hope I don't make it sound easy. I'm just trying to make it clear. Getting to this point takes a lot of practice.

Seem too hard? That's okay. You're not there yet. As you work the materials and exercises in this book, it will get easier over time.

7

....

The Panic Cycle

After a person has had a first panic attack, he will usually be suspicious and fearful of the situation in which he had that first attack. A person who had a first panic attack in a movie theater is probably not going to go back and see that particular movie, or go back to that particular theater, anytime soon.

Unfortunately, it usually doesn't stop there. People usually find that the anticipatory anxiety, and often the attacks themselves, spread to other situations and circumstances.

This leads people to fear that their lives are spinning out of control. People often describe their fear as irrational and random. The entire problem seems so illogical to them that they don't see how it can be solved.

If that were actually the case, that panic attacks occurred at random, it would make the task of recovery much more difficult. But the fact is that, for most people, there are rules which govern where and when they will experience recurrent panic attacks. It may seem random and irrational, but there is a logical set of rules that tell us where and when most recurrent attacks will occur.

It will help you in your recovery efforts to know what the rules are, so that you can be better prepared to work with them. You can also use these rules to identify the situations and activities you need to include in your exposure practice.

Recurrent panic attacks are likely to occur:

1. In situations that remind you of your first attack.

If you had your first panic attack in a large grocery store, for example, you will probably have some fears about going back to that particular store and, if it's part of a chain, about going to other stores in the chain. But, for many people, it won't stop there. You may find that you become uneasy about going to other large grocery stores as well. This fear may spread to other types of stores, for instance, large department stores and malls, even though you've never had an attack there.

You might avoid these stores, or you might still go but change your pattern of shopping in ways designed to avoid a panic attack. It's also common to associate panic with the time of day, or the kind of weather, that accompanied the first attack.

What situations or activities remind you of your first attack?

_____

_____

_____

_____

_____

_____

_____

_____

_____

_____

_____

_____

2. In situations that you see as a "trap."

When a person with panic disorder talks about a "trap," they usually mean any situation from which they can't leave as quickly, quietly, and invisibly as they may wish. They're on the lookout for such situations not only because having been sensitized by the first panic attack they naturally want to avoid recurrences, but also because they want to feel sure that they can leave any time they become anxious, without anyone noticing and asking about it. A supermarket line can seem like a trap, as can a divided highway, a red light, and the middle section of a church pew or movie theater.

What situations or activities do you think of as "traps"?

_____

_____

_____

_____

_____

3. In leisure-time activities and situations.

People tend to panic in situations in which they're bored or just killing time. Examples of this include watching a dull movie, waiting in a restaurant while your companion lingers over yet another cup of coffee, and sitting in a doctor's waiting room. They also include activities that don't really engage your mind because you can do them without much thinking, such as driving or taking a shower. Going to bed and waiting to fall asleep is another situation that gives a lot of people trouble.

During what leisure-time situations or activities do you get anxious because your mind is idle?

_____

_____

_____

_____

_____

4. When there is no emergency.

This is related to number 3 above. People tend not to panic "when the chips are down." Firemen who have panic attacks almost never have them during a fire when they're actually in danger. Instead, they tend to panic when they've been at the station for a long time without a fire, playing too much pinochle. If the fire bell does ring, the panic attack stops immediately. Parents rarely panic when their child falls down and breaks a nose or an arm. Instead, they typically take care of business, get their child treated at the ER, and don't start to feel panicky until after their child is safely home again.

The experience of recurrent panic attacks is not a random or mysterious process. Rather, it follows logical and consistent principles, even though they may lead to illogical fears. Understanding these rules can help you move from confusion to coping.

Understanding the Panic Cycle

Let's take a closer look at an individual panic attack. The better you understand the process and pattern of an individual panic attack, how physical sensations, thoughts, emotions, and behaviors interact to produce panic, the more able you will be to observe it, accept it, and wait for it to end without getting caught up in the turmoil it offers.

The first thing to notice, even before we consider the individual parts, is that the panic attack is cyclical. This is a big advantage. Why? Because it always follows the same, predictable pattern. A problem that keeps changing, that never follows the same pattern twice, is a very difficult problem to solve. A problem that follows the same pattern time and again is much easier to solve.

Many people with panic attacks don't realize that there is a pattern, and this makes their task of recovery much harder. They focus on the illogical or "irrational" aspects of the fears and fail to notice what a predictable pattern a panic attack follows.

They say things like "It doesn't make any sense...it's irrational," and give up on finding any logical pattern to the attacks. Naturally, this leads them to feel discouraged, because if they can't understand something, how can they change it? But, while it's true that the fears of a panic attack are exaggerated and unrealistic, the pattern a panic attack takes is predictable and regular. The symptoms often change over time, but the pattern remains the same. The diagram on page 78 depicts the stages of a panic attack.

A panic attack is a circular process and can be seen as starting at one of several points on the panic cycle. For our purposes, let's presume it starts with what I labeled the event. By *event*, I mean an anxiety symptom. The attack thus begins with an internal event, not something that takes place outside of you.

Recall a recent panic attack you experienced—one that you remember reasonably well, a strong one that scared you. What event (anxiety symptom) did you notice first?

_____

_____

_____

_____

However, you will note on the diagram that there is often an external *cue* that "triggers" the attack. For instance, as you drive toward an intersection where you want to turn left, you see a great big traffic jam, and you feel a lump develop in your throat, followed by a difficulty in breathing. The traffic jam is the cue; the physical symptoms are the event.

In the same attack you recalled above, did an external cue trigger the event in you? If so, what was it?

_____

_____

_____

How does a cue such as the traffic jam trigger a change in your body? Most often it will fill you with thoughts about the traffic jam, quick interpretations of what it means to you, and these will produce physical and emotional responses in you. These thoughts are largely beyond your voluntary control. You can't will yourself not to have them. If you're afraid of traffic jams (or dogs, or whatever), I assure you that you will have thoughts and mental images as soon as you see one. You may not consciously remember the thoughts, but they'll be there. Sometimes, you'll see a cue that appears to immediately mobilize your "fight or flight" response without ever producing a thought. But either way, the cue triggers the precipitating event of a panic attack.

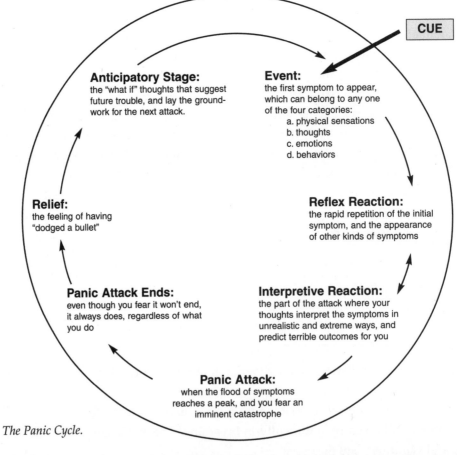

The Panic Cycle.

It's possible to have panic attacks both with, and without, a cue. People with panic disorder have probably experienced it both ways, having had attacks with and without an observable cue. As you become more "stuck" with the panic disorder, you will find that you no longer need an external cue to trigger a panic attack. It's often sufficient to just think of something you find threatening, or feel an unwelcome emotion like anger, and those thoughts and emotions serve as the cue. For example, people with a fear of heights can often experience panic symptoms just by thinking of a high, vulnerable situation, or by seeing a film in which such a scene is depicted.

In any event, the cue is much less important than what's happening inside you. The initial event could be any of the following:

1. a physical symptom (such as labored breathing, or feeling lightheaded)

2. a scary thought ("what if I have a panic attack at the party this weekend?")

3. an emotion (such as feeling angry or afraid)

4. or a behavior (such as holding your breath because you've been talking fast).

The event, then, is simply a panic symptom, the first one that comes to your attention as you start experiencing the first signs of a panic attack. This first symptom triggers the next part of the panic cycle: the *reflex reaction*. In a way that seems automatic and reflexive, you experience more of the first symptom you already experienced as the event. It's as if "one rapid heartbeat deserves another." And, like a landslide triggered by one rock falling down a slope, you start having more symptoms as well.

Many, but not all, of these additional symptoms are actually caused by your reaction to the event. For instance, if you start by feeling short of breath, you may tense up in ways that make your breathing even more labored...and the labored breathing will then begin to produce other symptoms, such as feeling dizzy or lightheaded.

In the same panic attack you described above, what reflex reaction (additional symptoms) was brought on by the initial event?

_____

_____

_____

_____

You might wonder, why do the symptoms start flooding over me this way? What produces this "avalanche" kind of effect?

This is what Dr. Claire Weekes, the renowned Australian anxiety expert, called "the second wave," and it usually feels worse than the first. This wave of additional symptoms occurs in response to the interaction between the reflex reaction and the next part of the cycle, the *interpretive reaction*.

The interpretive reaction is the part of the panic attack where you tell yourself what the symptoms mean for you. This is the "guess" that I referred to earlier. In some way, consciously or unconsciously, you decide what the symptoms of the event and reflex reaction mean, that is, you make an interpretation of those symptoms. Most of the time, this interpretation will be some form of this thought: "uh oh, I'm in trouble." This is the proverbial "fear of fear" you hear so much about.

In the same panic attack you described above, what interpretive reaction (thoughts about your symptoms) was brought on by the event and your reflex reaction to it?

_____

_____

_____

_____

_____

Notice that the arrows in the diagram between the reflex reaction and the interpretative reaction are pointing both ways. This indicates that these stages interact and affect each other. What happens between the two reactions is a two-way street. The interpretations of danger and illness lead to more physical symptoms, and the physical symptoms give rise to more scary interpretations.

The interpretive reaction is usually an anticipation of doom. For instance, a person might see an airplane overhead and picture himself on board a plane, having a panic attack, and acting like a crazy person. That's an interpretive reaction. All that really happened is that he saw an airplane. But in response, he experienced some involuntary thoughts that reflect his fear. When he instinctively

---

The Meaning of "Unconscious"

Before I go any further, let me explain what I mean by "unconscious," because that term means different things to different people, and can often be confusing. I use it in a very simple way to describe thoughts, feelings and sensations of which I am unaware, or that I don't notice when they occur. For instance, as you read this now, you have probably not been consciously aware of the sensation of the floor beneath your feet...

...but now you are.

THE PANIC CYCLE 81

resists these thoughts, he produces more reflex reaction symptoms—muscular tension, labored breathing, and so on. That, in turn, leads to an even more catastrophic interpretive reaction ("Oh NO! It's happening again!") and thus keeps the cycle moving along. If nothing else intervenes, these two reactions escalate and fuel each other, creating more fear—and fear of fear—and culminating in the peak of the *panic attack*.

At last the *panic attack ends*. It always does. You retain your life and your sanity despite the terror you experienced.

And yet, how many times have you had a panic attack and had this thought: "What if it never ends?" This kind of thought makes the panic attack feel worse if you don't have the right answer.

And the right answer is: "This panic attack will end because they all end. It's not up to me to end the attack. This panic attack will end regardless of what I do. Whether I do everything the best way possible to calm me down, or the worst way possible to get myself more agitated, the panic attack will end. It is not my job to end the attack. My only job is to make myself as comfortable as possible while waiting for the attack to end."

How do I know that's true for you? It's true for everyone I've ever met who had panic attacks. You can tell if it's true for you. Review your own history. Have you had any attacks that didn't end?

Take a few minutes to consider the answer above, and compare it to your own history and experience.

Is this answer true for you?   ❑ Yes   ❑ No

If you checked "no," this answer is not true for you because:

_____

_____

_____

_____

_____

If this answer is not true for you, I suggest you review this aspect of your panic with a professional therapist.

When the panic attack ends, as they all do, you feel *relief*. You're glad it's over. It's common to feel tired and drained, as if you just ran a hard race. You might have other reactions as well, either positive or negative, depending on your experience and the interpretation you put on it. You may feel embarrassed or ashamed for getting so afraid. You may feel angry that it happened again. You may feel depressed by the reminder that your life is so easily turned upside down. Or, if you had some good results with your belly breathing, or some other helpful technique, you may feel encouraged, and proud of your effort.

In the same panic attack you described above, what positive emotions did you experience after the attack ended?

_____

_____

_____

_____

_____

What negative emotions did you experience?

_____

_____

_____

_____

_____

But at some point—maybe the next hour, maybe the next day, maybe the next week, it's bound to happen that you'll experience some "what if" thinking, and enter into the *anticipatory stage* of the cycle. It's here that you start dreading the next appearance of panic, or panic symptoms, and hoping that they don't return. Once you've started worrying about a symptom or situation, it's easy to produce another event, and you're off again, into the vicious, repetitive cycle of panic.

This is why I said that the panic attack could begin at several places on the cycle. It makes just as much sense to see one starting in the anticipatory stage, as it does to see it starting with the event itself. They're all points on a loop, constantly cycling through the same pattern.

How does the panic cycle described in this chapter compare to your experience of panic? Are there any important differences?

_____

_____

_____

_____

Does the model describe your experience reasonably well? If not, why not?

_____

_____

_____

_____

_____

If the model doesn't adequately describe some aspect of your panic attacks, how would you modify it to better fit your experience?

_____

_____

_____

_____

_____

Breaking the Panic Cycle

If you're satisfied that the panic cycle I've described here is a reasonable description of the way you experience panic attacks, then you can use it to figure out how you can break the panic cycle.

First, answer these questions.

At a time when you were starting to panic, have you ever been interrupted by a surprise visit from a good friend, an important phone call, a child falling down and getting hurt, or some other unexpected event that demanded your attention?   ❑ Yes   ❑ No

Did you later remember that you had been starting to panic, and realize that the panic attack simply ended when you were interrupted?   ❑ Yes   ❑ No

Most people with panic have had these kinds of experiences. If you have, use the following questions to create a brief description of your experience.

I was at _____ doing _____. I noticed the following symptom(s) that made me think I was starting to panic:

_____

_____

_____

Then, the following unexpected event occurred:

_____

_____

_____

_____

_____

The result of this interruption was:

_____

_____

_____

_____

_____

Most people with panic have found connections between their thoughts and the panic. For instance, maybe as they were entering a large grocery store, they had the thought "what if I have a panic attack in here?" and were so frightened and upset by that thought that they had a panic attack almost immediately. Or maybe they've noticed that sometimes, when they get distracted from panic, it fades more quickly. This often leads people to think along this line: "If I don't think about it, I won't panic." So they try to distract themselves from panic by avoiding the subject entirely, in the hope that by so doing, they can protect themselves from panic.

Unfortunately, this can cause you a lot of trouble. There are a couple of problems with it. It's certainly true that, at least under certain circumstances, a distraction can interrupt and stop a panic attack. But the kind of distraction that can help you most is distraction that comes from an outside source—the kind that results from somebody else doing something that distracts you. The problem is, you can't count on a distraction being available whenever you want one.

Fear of Burritos

I worked for a while with a client who was in the habit of eating a lot of heavy food, such as burritos. Sometimes he would get a severe burst of indigestion and discomfort in his stomach an hour or so after one of his heavy lunches. His instinctive reaction was that this was some sign of physical disease, like a tumor. No sooner did the thought of a tumor cross his mind than he was off and running with a panic attack.

Those of you who aren't so used to eating this way might think it would be easy to recognize what was going on. But he was used to eating this way, had eaten this way most of his life, and no longer made direct connections between how he was eating and how his stomach felt. After we discovered this pattern (thanks to his use of panic diaries), he was able to stop and recognize that there were numerous possible explanations for his stomach upset. He trained himself to review these possibilities before coming to any conclusions about the source of his stomach upset.

Realizing that the scary thoughts he experienced were only his instinctive guess, rather than a reliable warning of danger that was always accurate, helped him reshape his responses to the fear.

People often try to distract themselves. This doesn't work as well, because when you do it, you know why you're trying to distract yourself, and from what. The inner dialogue, or self talk, of someone trying to distract herself or himself goes something like this.

"Stop thinking about it!"

"Hmmm, stop thinking about what?"

"Aauugghhh! You're thinking about it again!"

Try this:

For the next ten seconds, do not think about elephants. What happened?

_____

_____

_____

There are some real limitations to how useful distraction can be as a strategy for coping with panic. The more deliberately you try to use it—the more consciously you choose to distract yourself—the less likely it is to work. Aside from the fact that it doesn't work reliably, there are other reasons to not rely on distraction.

The idea behind distraction is that, if you don't think about panic, you won't panic. This often leads people to assume that thinking about panic is enough to cause a panic attack. It's not that simple. Such an assumption can mislead you.

Have you ever pulled out a bottle of Xanax (or some other medication) when you were feeling panicky and felt better just by looking at it?   ❏ Yes   ❏ No

Have you taken a Xanax (or some other medication) and gotten instant relief as soon as you took one, even before it could actually take effect? ❏ Yes   ❏ No

If you haven't used these medications, have you ever started having a panic attack and then your "safe person" arrived, or called you on your cellular phone, and you started to feel better because of it?   ❏ Yes   ❏ No

Have you ever started to panic and found that it ended as you pulled out some written material about panic, such as this book or your own written observations?   ❏ Yes   ❏ No

In such instances, people often start to feel better even though they clearly haven't been distracted from the subject of panic. When they see or take the Xanax, they know it's a medication for panic attacks. When they see their safe person, they know that this person helps them not panic somehow. When they review their panic materials, they're reminded of certain aspects of panic.

They're thinking about panic, rather than being distracted from it—and yet they feel better. That's because they're not thinking about the panic *in a particular kind of way*. Their viewpoint has changed. They're thinking about the panic from an observer's point of view rather than a victim's. And by thinking about it in a more realistic, less catastrophic way, they are no longer engaging in phobic self talk.

What Is Self Talk?

Self talk is simply the process of thinking to yourself, about the world and your place in it. We do this all day long, every day of the year, every year of our adult lives, often without even noticing it. We probably all learned to do it in a similar way, even though we don't remember the process because we were too young.

One of the most important characteristics of self talk is that it's subliminal. In other words, you hear it as a background sound, without paying a lot of attention to it. Because you don't pay much attention to it, it has more influence with you, because you don't notice what you're telling yourself, and therefore don't usually challenge or analyze it.

But even when you're not paying close attention to your self talk, your body will still "get the message." And that brings up another important characteristic of self talk. Your body will respond as if it were true, even when it isn't. This is okay when your self talk is reasonably positive, or realistic; but can cause you lots of trouble when your self talk is negative and unrealistic. I'll show you:

Imagine a lemon.

Close your eyes and imagine holding a yellow lemon in your hands. Feel the two different ends of the lemon. Feel the texture of the skin of the lemon. Hold the lemon under your nose and smell it. Cut the lemon open and smell it again. Taste the juice that gets on your fingers.

If you're like most people, you don't have to do too much of this before you notice some extra saliva in your mouth. That's produced just by thinking about the lemon. You don't actually have to taste a lemon to produce extra saliva. You don't have to travel halfway across town to actually get a lemon. Simply picturing it in your mind is enough to get your body to produce some extra saliva to help digest it.

What we think about and visualize in our minds can have effects on what we actually experience physically. Our thoughts and self talk are not just idle chatter. They can, and do, influence our physical experience.

Phobic Self Talk

Phobic self talk is the kind of thinking and talking to oneself that sets the stage for panic attacks. It's full of suggestions and innuendoes, some subtle and some not so subtle, which are continually offering a subliminal influence to keep the person in a state of anticipatory panic. It has three characteristics:

- It's unrealistic.
- It's negative.
- It's persistent.

Phobic self talk comes into play at two key parts of the panic cycle: the interpretive reaction and the anticipatory stage. These are the two parts of the cycle where you can benefit the most from observing and working with your thoughts.

Phobic self talk in the interpretive reaction consists principally of misinterpreting discomfort for danger. It's here, for instance, when you feel dizzy or lightheaded, that you might hear yourself thinking it means you're about to faint, when it really means that you're breathing too short and shallow, or maybe holding your breath. It's also here that you might feel tightness or pressure in your chest and hear yourself thinking that it means a heart attack, when it really means that you've tightened up your chest muscles with shallow breathing. You might find yourself getting disoriented by your own racing thoughts and hear yourself thinking that it means you're "losing it," when it really means that you're upset and confused.

Power of Suggestion

Here's an example of what I mean from my own life. I had occasion, while living in Chicago, to paint the interior walls of my condo. I had a big window, floor to ceiling, in my living room. I painted all the other walls just fine, using a step ladder to get the top of the wall. When it came time to paint the trim around the window, I remember thinking it would not be a good time to trip or stumble on the ladder, because I'd probably crash through the glass and down four flights onto the parking lot. The entire time I was painting, I was very conscious of the need not to trip. I survived. But when I finished that wall, and got down off the ladder, guess what happened?

If you guessed that I tripped, once I was safely on the floor, you're right. And I think it's reasonable to conclude that it had to do with the fact that "tripping" was on my mind the entire time I was on the ladder painting. It was such a powerful self-suggestion to myself to not trip that, once I was no longer in a vulnerable position, all that thinking about not tripping persisted until I actually did trip.

Now, would everybody in that situation, painting around a big window overlooking a parking lot, have the same reaction? No. There are probably lots of people who wouldn't give it a second thought. There are probably some people who wouldn't get on the ladder at all. And there's me, with a sufficiently mild fear of heights to allow me to get on a simple stepladder, but not without such thoughts.

The key in that type of situation is to recognize the thoughts as signs of nervousness, not danger.

Or you might be making more global generalizations about yourself and what's happening to you. If you could listen in to someone's thoughts as they were having a panic attack, you'd probably hear some of the following:

- "I can't stand it!"
- "Everybody is watching me and wondering what's wrong!"
- "I'm trapped!"
- "I have to get out of here!"

What are some of the misinterpretations you hear in your thoughts in the interpretive reaction stage of a panic cycle?

_____

_____

_____

_____

Phobic self talk in the anticipatory stage consists mostly of "what if" messages about terrible things you imagine might happen to you, such as:

- "What if I have a heart attack?"
- "What if I faint?"
- "What if I freak out?"
- "What if I freak out and drive off the bridge?"
- "What if I freak out and abandon my car and start running down the highway?"
- "What if I start screaming in that very quiet and sedate jewelry store?"
- "What if the neighbors invite me to their daughter's wedding reception?"

This is often called anticipatory worry. There's a simple formula for this type of thinking, and it goes like this.

Say "what if." Then fill in the blank with something terrible. Most people with panic and phobias think this way a lot. How about you?

What are some of the "what if" thoughts you notice in your self talk before, or during, a panic attack?

What if _____ ?

What if _____ ?

What if _____ ?

What if _____ ?

What if _____ ?

Some people say they never have such thoughts. I guess it's possible, but I think a more likely explanation is that they're so used to this kind of self talk that they don't pay it much conscious attention. But self talk doesn't need conscious attention to have the effect of scaring you and starting up the panic cycle.

If you're like most people with panic and phobias, that means you're regularly experiencing thoughts predicting personal catastrophes that don't tend to occur. Sometimes these thoughts are subliminal and automatic. They create in you an anxious mood without your understanding where it comes from. Sometimes the thoughts are loud and obvious, and you become embroiled in an argument with them, or you struggle to distract yourself from them.

Fill in the blanks:

Every time I see (or visit) a _____,
                                          (object or place)

I think of the time I panicked at _____
                                          (location of previous panic attack)

_____.

That's when I started feeling _____
                                          (physical sensations)

and became afraid that I was about to _____
                                          (catastrophe you feared then)

_____.

When I remember that now, I find myself thinking, "What if

_____?"
                                          (catastrophe you anticipate now)

Now can you add some more?

_____

_____

_____

_____

_____

_____

_____

_____

_____

Imagine how your body will respond to hearing these dire thoughts. Remember, your body is kind of an innocent, naive being. It's going to respond to whatever it hears as if it were true, regardless of how true or false it actually is. Your body will produce almost as much saliva for an imaginary lemon as for a real one. It will produce the same fear on a roller coaster that it would if you fell off a roof. So when your body hears these insinuations about disaster, what's it going to do? Is it liable to remain cool, calm, and collected, knowing that it's just hearing the empty threats and false predictions of the anticipatory stage of the panic cycle . . . or not?

Thinking back to the panic attack you were describing in the exercises earlier in this chapter, what did your body experience?

_____

_____

_____

_____

_____

If you find yourself in the same circumstances in the future, do you imagine that your body will experience the same sensations?   ❏ Yes   ❏ No
Why or why not?

_____

_____

_____

_____

When you talk to yourself about catastrophic consequences, it's only natural that your body is going to trigger its emergency responses and flood you with adrenaline, speed up your heart, and make you feel like fleeing. That would be

Welcome Changes

Once you learn how to get the practice you need, and actually get that practice, you will notice some changes appear in your life:

- You'll notice that the average severity of your panic attacks becomes less and less.
- You'll notice that the average length of time in between panic attacks becomes longer and longer.
- You'll notice that the average duration of a panic attack becomes shorter and shorter.
- You'll notice that your use of avoidance and other "self-protective" methods gradually declines.
- And your fear of fear will gradually diminish.
- And finally, when you lose your fear of the attacks, that's when they fade away.

great if there really were an emergency, because it would give you the energy and motivation you need to protect yourself. But since there's no real danger to run from, it's only going to make you feel worse.

People often underestimate the power of their mind to create panic attacks and think of them as a purely biological phenomenon. "Aren't they due to a chemical imbalance?" is a question I hear frequently.

Certainly there are chemical aspects to a panic attack, because we are literally made of chemicals. It's also true that the use of certain chemicals in panic medications can often help people. But the "chemical imbalance" explanation overlooks some of the most important aspects of chronic panic disorder. Here's an exercise to help clarify this.

Write down two situations in which you think you're almost guaranteed to have a panic attack.

1. _____

_____

_____

2. _____

_____

_____

Now write down two situations in which you would be extremely unlikely to have a panic attack.

1. _____

_____

_____

2. _____

_____

_____

Now, here's the question to consider:

How do the chemicals find out where you are?

If you're like most people, you tell them with your self talk. That's how the chemicals "find out." You can learn how to talk to yourself differently and send the chemicals a message that all is well.

Exiting the Panic Cycle

Let's turn our attention back to the panic cycle. If you're like most people, you've had incidents when you started to panic, but interrupted it yourself by something you did or thought, or had it interrupted by the actions of others. These interruptions are actually common occurrences.

Even once a panic attack starts, you don't always automatically follow through with a full-blown attack. Depending on what you do, how you respond to the initial stages of the attack, you might go on to have a full attack, or you might skip it entirely. It's not a command performance.

What I've called the *event* really deserves a different name. It's an *invitation* to a panic attack, not a command. Depending on how you respond to the invitation,

The Worst Thing about Dentists . . .

I worked with a woman, let's call her Diane, who had many phobias as part of a diagnosis of panic disorder. Over time, she overcame her fear of driving, of elevators, of shopping, of going to the doctor and numerous other fears. But despite our best efforts, she remained unable to go to the dentist. I couldn't really figure out why.

Finally, one day she said this to me. "The thing I hate most about going to the dentist is when they chain you into the chair."

My first thought, when she said this, was that I was going to be spending some time in front of the Dental Regulatory Board, testifying against this dentist from hell who chained his patients into the chair.

Then I realized she was talking about the bib.

The bib does have a piece of chain on it. And they do put that chain on you when you sit in the chair. But they don't actually chain you into the chair. That's there for comfort and cleanliness, not confinement.

Of course, she knew that. But she also thought of the dentist's chair as a trap, from which there was no escape unless and until the dentist said she could leave. Many people feel this way about the dentist. These thoughts, operating in the background, kept her anxious enough about the dentist that she was unable to make an appointment.

With this out in the open, our next step was to help her feel more in control of herself during her time in the dental chair. She arranged to talk to the dentist, and told him about her panic attacks, and her need to be able to take a break during dental procedures. They worked out some hand signals she could use. This gave her enough sense of control that she was able to schedule, and attend, her first dental appointment in many years.

Thoughts—however reasonable or unreasonable—really do count.

you may or may not "go to the party." If you take the phobic self talk seriously, and get into a struggle to make it go away, you're probably "going to the party." But if you recognize the phobic self talk for the trash talking it is, and observe these thoughts without getting embroiled in a struggle, you're probably going to skip it.

What actually happens—whether you panic or don't panic—depends on how you respond to the invitation. When you don't talk to yourself in a negative, scary, and unrealistic way and when you don't struggle to protect yourself, you generally don't panic. Instead, you cope and exit the cycle.

But when you take your phobic self talk at face value and struggle to protect yourself, you're likely to panic. Your body will respond to the phobic self talk as if it were true, even if it's not.

This invitation to panic, and the choices you face in responding to the invitation, are depicted in the drawing below.

An essential ingredient to panic attacks is the unrealistic, scary, misinterpretation of what's going on around you, and especially within you. As we've seen, when you get distracted from this scary self talk, or when you're with a "safe per-

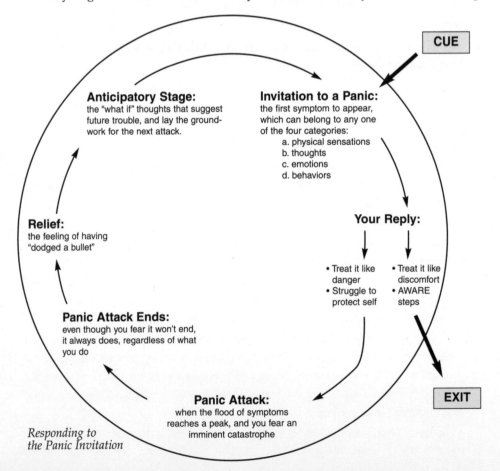

Responding to the Panic Invitation

son," you don't panic. But you can't always count on a distraction occurring or your safe person being there.

If you could find some other way to change the scary self talk, you'd have a better, more reliable way of preventing panic. That means you'd get over panic attacks. All you have to do is get rid of the phobic self talk and you'll get rid of the panic.

Pretty good, huh?

But, there's a catch.

Once you've been sensitized by a panic attack, you probably can't just dismiss it. If it were that easy, you'd have already done so, and you wouldn't be reading this book.

Practice, Practice, Practice

When you suspect that your life or sanity is on the line, you need something other than positive self talk to help you. Nothing anybody else might say will be enough. You need to tell yourself something you know to be true from your own personal experience. When you hear that question "what if I have a panic attack?" the only answer sufficiently powerful to help you calm down will be something like "that's okay, if I panic here I'll do the same thing I did the last time. That worked pretty well." Your own reminder that you know how to interrupt a panic attack is the only thing that will be strong enough to regularly put the panic attack to rest. And there's only one way to get that. You need practice coping with panic. That's the catch.

You need practice in coping with the sensations of panic—gradual, progressive practice that will help you determine for yourself over time that you are safe. As you come to believe you can cope, from your own practice, you will begin to talk yourself out of the attacks.

You would probably prefer to find a method that helps you recover without ever again feeling the sensations of panic. Who wouldn't? Yet this is just another way panic tricks you. While you're waiting for a new miracle drug to be invented, or for the panic disorder to disappear on its own, the panic is becoming a more deeply ingrained habit in your life.

The method that's been shown to be most effective for panic attacks and phobias is called "exposure therapy"—that is, exposure to panic so that you can practice responding to it. This will enable you to develop a new answer to the question, "what if I have a panic attack?" The answer that will work will be some variation of "I'll do what I did the last time I panicked. That seemed to work pretty well."

It's a lot like learning self-defense. If you went to a self-defense class and took copious notes and observed carefully but never participated in the practice sparring, you wouldn't learn much self-defense. You certainly wouldn't develop any confidence in your self-defense abilities. To develop self-defense skills, and confidence in those skills, you would literally need to practice fighting with the other students and the instructor.

It's the same with panic. To develop your coping skills, and your confidence in them, you literally need to practice with panic.

PART TWO

LAYING THE GROUNDWORK FOR RECOVERY

8

....

Secrecy and Self-Disclosure

Who knows about the trouble you have with panic attacks and anxiety?
Make a list. Who really knows about it?

_____

_____

_____

_____

_____

_____

If you're like most people with panic, there probably aren't too many others who know. Most people try to keep their panic attacks a secret, and this is another part of the panic trick. Let's take a look at the role secrecy plays in this problem.

People make up a lot of excuses to keep their panic a secret. When they receive an invitation or request to go somewhere or do something that might result in a panic attack, they think up reasons to justify saying "no." Of course, they could simply say "I don't want to do that. I've been having trouble with panic attacks, and I think I might have one if I go to that restaurant." But most people with panic attacks feel too ashamed and embarrassed to say it so plainly. They often think that if people knew about their trouble, they would probably think less of them—maybe think they're "crazy."

They may also fear that if they bring their panic to other people's attention, the problem may somehow worsen. For instance, they don't want someone asking them every five minutes, "Are you okay?" because that would probably make them anxious. Or they don't want to mention the panic attacks to others because "It's none of their business."

Keeping panic hidden comes so naturally that many people never consider an alternative to the secrecy and deception. They just assume, without thinking it through, that it's the only thing to do. When they do realize that there's another way, they're often surprised. "You mean…just be honest?"

It's true that your panic attacks are no one's business but yours. The key is to conduct your business in a way that will maximize your recovery. If you decide to tell anyone about your panic, the reason won't be because they deserve to know about it but rather because telling them will help promote your recovery.

Let's consider how people use secrecy and deception, and the results it actually produces for them. Here are some typical examples:

- You accept a date to attend a party. You like this person, but you worry that you might feel "trapped" there and that your date might not want to leave early. You make up an excuse that requires you to bring separate cars so that you have a guaranteed way to leave if you feel panicky.
- Your boss asks you to present your work at an upcoming staff meeting and you agree, but secretly you plan on calling in sick when the day arrives. You leave detailed notes in your desk so that someone else can use them to brief the group.

In each case, the excuse gives you an "out." That might make it seem like a success. But just as most medications have some kind of side effects, some harmless and some harmful, the use of secrecy and deception has consequences as well.

Side Effect One: Imagining the Worst

One consequence of secrecy is that you never find out how people would actually react to your secret. Instead, you *imagine* how they would react. If you're like most people with an anxiety disorder, you tend to imagine the worst possible scenarios, the grimmest "what if" outcomes, such as envisioning that other people will react with disgust and ridicule on hearing about your fear. As a result, you end up with the emotional feelings that fit your dire prediction—not the reality. Your body and mind react to your own worst predictions just as if they were true even though if you asked, your friend would tell you honestly that they have no basis in fact.

The truth is, when you begin to break the secrecy, your friends will react in much more positive and supportive ways than you anticipated. The side effect of your secrecy, then, is that that you systematically feel *worse* about yourself than you would if you were more open about your problem. Your secrecy and excuses solve no problems, but rather maintain them and even make them worse.

Write down the name of a close friend or relative who does not know about your panic attacks. _____

How Embarrassment Can Help the Panic Sufferer

What does it mean if you have a panic attack, and feel embarrassed about it?

This is a common occurrence. A person having a panic attack during a luncheon out with a friend might try to hide that fact and end the lunch early without revealing his distress. A person traveling with another in a car might try to endure the panic attack until he reaches his destination rather than ask the driver to pull over. It's very much a part of the typical panic experience to feel embarrassed about having a panic attack and try to hide it.

This can be a powerful signal to use for your own constructive purposes.

When you feel embarrassed in the context of a panic attack, it's because you recognize that there is "no good reason" to feel so afraid, that your fear is excessive and unreasonable. You realize that you're not really in danger, and yet you're afraid anyway.

This is a very helpful form of feedback. When you feel embarrassed in response to a panic attack, it's a reminder that you're up against discomfort, not danger. You can use this embarrassment as a signal, a reminder to yourself that what you need to do now is treat the panic as the discomfort it is. That means accepting the panic and working with it.

How do you imagine that friend would react if you told him or her about your attacks today?

_____

_____

_____

_____

_____

If the situation were reversed, and your friend suddenly revealed to you that he or she has been suffering from recurrent panic attacks, how would you react?

_____

_____

_____

_____

With that in mind, do you still think your secrecy is justified?_____

Side Effect Two: Feel Like a Fraud

Another consequence is that, when you hold what you consider to be a "dark" secret, you tend to discount your accomplishments and relationships with others. It's easy to believe that if people "knew the truth" about you, they wouldn't like you as much, or respect you as much, or want to be your friend. If you think you've been fooling people, it's hard to take comfort in your accomplishments or relationships.

The irony is that it's usually the people with the secret, not their friends, who are getting fooled. They're usually good, accomplished, likable people. Their phobias, however problematic, don't change their worth as a person. But they won't understand that until they break the secrecy by telling people about their problem, and realizing that they're still accepted and valued.

If you asked your friend or relative right now whether he or she thinks you are a good, accomplished, likeable person, what do you think they would say?

_____

_____

_____

_____

What accomplishments and virtues might he or she point out in support of their opinion of you?

_____

_____

_____

_____

If you revealed your secret panic attacks, which of these accomplishments and virtues would he or she be likely to change their mind about?

_____

_____

_____

Side Effect Three: Increased Worry and Anxiety

A third problem with secrecy is that, when you do go somewhere with people, you may be so concerned with protecting your secret and keeping others from noticing your fear that you can't fully enjoy the occasion. A kind of stage fright—"what if I don't play my role well?"—can contribute to your perception of being "trapped," making you miserable, anxious, and more likely to have a panic attack.

For example, when some people venture out to a restaurant, they assure themselves that if they become very anxious, they can excuse themselves and go to the bathroom, maybe splashing some cold water on their face, and being alone for a few minutes. But they also worry, what if they have to visit the bathroom more than once? Won't their companion wonder what's wrong? They're so intent on avoiding this potential attention that they decide to limit themselves to one bathroom visit. Then they decide they have to save that visit for a "real emergency," so in effect, they can't visit the bathroom at all. Their effort at secrecy ends up making them feel more trapped and prone to panic.

Can you think of any ways in which your "escape routes" actually end up making you feel more trapped?

_____

_____

_____

_____

_____

Side Effect Four: Social Isolation

Yet another problem, of course, is that if you fall into a habit of making excuses as a way to decline invitations, your friends are going to notice. If you do it consistently, after a while people will form their own ideas about why you keep turning them down. If they don't know the real reason, they're likely to guess that you don't enjoy their company, and may abandon their efforts to stay in touch with you. Then you can become socially isolated and more stuck in your phobias.

Think back on a recent incident in which you made up an excuse to avoid a situation with a friend, rather than reveal that panic was the reason you didn't want to go. Who invited you, and to what?

_____

_____

_____

What excuse did you offer?

_____

_____

_____

_____

How did your friend react?

_____

_____

_____

How did you feel emotionally?

_____

_____

_____

_____

Did you experience any of the side effects described above? Which? To what extent?

_____

_____

_____

_____

_____

   Except in highly unusual cases, I recommend breaking out of secrecy. Most people are better able to take care of the business of recovery when they replace secrecy with selective self-disclosure. That doesn't mean you have to tell everybody you know all about your troubles. Instead, take two deliberate steps:

- Identify those situations and relationships in which self-disclosure could help you in your recovery, or in some other important aspect of life, such as maintaining friendships.
- With each person you choose to reveal your condition to, plan ahead and be deliberate in deciding what to disclose and how to do it.

Evaluate the Costs and Benefits of Selective Disclosure

Here's an exercise that will guide you through the first step. Think of three friends or family members who you know have your best interests at heart. Because self-disclosure is a learning process, start with people who are genuinely supportive of you. For now, don't be concerned with their ability to understand the problem, only with the quality of their relationship to you. Identify the first person below, and answer each question about that person.

Name_____

What are the benefits of keeping the secret?

_____

_____

_____

_____

_____

What are the negative side effects of keeping the secret?

_____

_____

_____

_____

_____

What are the potential benefits of disclosure?

_____

_____

_____

_____

_____

What are the potential negative side effects of disclosure?

_____

_____

_____

_____

_____

Use this outline to identify and evaluate the costs and benefits of keeping secrets about your panic and phobias from a friend or relative. Try to define the actual risks and troubles, not just emotional discomfort. For instance, you might think that you will "feel embarrassed" if you disclose anything about your troubles. But feeling embarrassed, however unpleasant, is only an emotion, and a temporary one at that. People sometimes equate feeling embarrassed with some kind of breakdown, or a crying jag that lasts forever. But if you anticipate a negative emotional reaction to telling someone about your panic problem, try to pinpoint what the result of that negative emotion will be.

By the same token, "feeling good" about yourself as a result of self-disclosure doesn't tell the whole story either. If telling someone about your problem helps you feel better, what concrete events or changes might that lead to?

Boil the costs and benefits down to real outcomes, not just emotions. When you identify an emotion as an outcome, ask yourself "and if I feel that way, what will be the results of that feeling?" and do that until you find the actual results, if any.

Use this exercise to consider several people for possible self-disclosure. The reason to do any self-disclosure, remember, is to achieve a benefit for yourself, something that will help you in your recovery efforts. Hopefully, you will find several people with whom a candid discussion might be of benefit to you.

Name_____

What are the benefits of keeping the secret?

_____

_____

_____

_____

_____

What are the negative side effects of keeping the secret?

_____

_____

_____

_____

_____

What are the potential benefits of disclosure?

_____

_____

_____

_____

_____

What are the potential negative side effects of disclosure?

_____

_____

_____

_____

_____

Name_____

What are the benefits of keeping the secret?

_____

_____

_____

_____

_____

What are the negative side effects of keeping the secret?

_____

_____

_____

_____

_____

What are the potential benefits of disclosure?

_____

_____

_____

_____

What are the potential negative side effects of disclosure?

_____

_____

_____

_____

Using Self-Disclosure

If you decide it's in your best interest to do some selective disclosure, here are some suggestions for how to go about it.

First, tell the person you have something to discuss, and schedule a time. Don't try to work it into a casual conversation as if it just occurred to you. The best way is to phone your friend or family member and tell him or her that you'd like to get together and talk something over. Plan on an hour or so, so neither of you feels rushed by other commitments. Pick a place where you have sufficient privacy. It's okay to schedule it around a meal or beverages (nonalcoholic only) if you like, but nothing so extensive it gets in the way of your primary purpose. Or plan your conversation around a walk so you can keep moving as you talk. If your friend wants to know what the topic is, simply explain that there are a few things going on with you that you'd like to talk about, or words to that effect. Don't be terribly mysterious, but stay with your plan to schedule the conversation, rather than have it right then and there on the phone.

When you get together, get to your topic as soon as reasonable. To avoid building up anxiety, keep small talk to a minimum. Your friend may wait for you to bring it up. Get right to it, even though you'll naturally feel anxious. Allow yourself to have whatever reaction you have. Resistance will simply make it worse. If you think you're likely to cry, bring plenty of tissues.

Here's a typical introduction you can adapt to your own purposes:

> "Thanks for coming over. I wanted to talk with you because I'm having a little trouble. There's something going on with me, and I think it will help me just to talk about it a little so I'm not carrying this big secret around. I'm not dying, and I don't want to borrow any money. There isn't really anything I'm going to ask you to do, it'll just be good to not have this secret.
>
> "You might have noticed I've been avoiding some things lately, for example, _____. It's because I've been having panic attacks. Do you know anything about panic attacks?"

Then explain a bit about panic attacks and how they affect you, and how they lead you to avoid certain activities. People who have never experienced a panic attack frequently find it hard to understand so here's a suggestion. Most people seem to understand what claustrophobia is all about. They usually "get" the idea of someone who becomes terribly, unreasonably afraid in a small enclosed space. So you can explain that it's like claustrophobia, not specifically related to small spaces, but that you feel something similar to claustrophobia in other conditions that are crowded, or difficult to leave (like highways), or whatever kinds of circumstances are triggers for you. You might suggest some books and websites where they can find additional information (see Resources at the end of this book). But remember, your friends don't have to understand perfectly. The self-disclosure is for your benefit, not theirs.

When your friend wants to know what he or she can do to help, explain that most importantly if you become afraid while in their company you want to feel free to say you're having trouble, instead of having to hide it. They don't have to do anything, just be responsive if you ask them for help or understanding at that time. You want them to know it's not a physical emergency, and they don't need to look at you all the time, asking if you're okay. In short, you're telling them this so you don't have to carry the secret around but can be yourself with them.

Once you've broken the ice with this person, you'll be free to handle the threat of panic differently in the future. For instance, if you're at a restaurant with this friend, once you no longer need to be secretive, you could let her or him know that, if you have a panic attack, you might need to excuse yourself to visit the bathroom, take a walk in the parking lot, or even end the meal if necessary, and you could explain what you would, and wouldn't, want them to do under those circumstances. That will help you feel less trapped, and aware of better options, so you'll be much less likely to panic.

Working with a Support Person

Most people who have panic attacks have discovered that they can venture further outside of their "safe zone" and "safe activities" when they are accompanied by a "support person" (also called a "safe person"). If you avoid certain kinds of roads, or large crowded stores, you might be able to tolerate them when your support person goes with you. Many people who are afraid of flying find that even though they are afraid to fly by themselves, they can manage a trip if their support person goes along. People with panic are usually still afraid with a support person along and still put limitations on what they do and where they go, but the limitations are loosened a little bit.

You might be in a situation you fear—a grocery store, for example—in the company of your support person. He or she goes off to the cereal aisle while you shop in oils and vinegars. As you're looking for a good olive oil, you feel a wave of panic. Your breathing becomes labored. Just as you start entering into a full-blown panic attack, your support person comes around the corner carrying a box of bran flakes with raisins. You feel better instantly and continue shopping together.

It seems like a miracle, but the truth is, a support person doesn't have to do anything other than be there. In fact, a hologram or mirage of your support person would do just as well. A support person is really just a special kind of "support object," like a water bottle or an old bottle of Xanax. He or she is like a portable billboards reminding you, "You're gonna be okay!"

The relief and calming effect you feel comes from you, not the support person. It's like the relationship between a band and the bandleader. The bandleader gives the signal to start, but the band plays the music. Your support person gives you the signal to relax, but you do the relaxing.

Unfortunately, most people with panic don't recognize or believe that. They treat the support person as a magical source of safety. So long as they do this, and aren't able to recognize that they're the source of their own comfort, not the support person, they continue to feel vulnerable and dependent on others. This keeps them phobic, and more likely to have recurrent panic attacks.

Most people who use support objects and support people think of them as helpful rather than harmful—and they are helpful, in the short run. But long-term reliance on a support person will delay, perhaps block, your recovery.

Text continued on page 112.

Support Person Ground Rules

Here are some ground rules to make your work with a support person as productive as possible. If you're already working with a support person, evaluate that relationship to see how well you're following these guidelines. If you're following them all, great. Your work with that support person will probably be positive and productive for you. If not, review these guidelines with your support person and try to make changes in the way you work together.

1. You make all the decisions, not the support person.

You're in charge. The support person is second banana. Regardless of whether or not your decision is consistent with the principles of progressive exposure (see Part Three), all decisions are yours to make, not your support person's. If you decide to cut short an exposure session because you don't feel up to it that day, this is a departure from the principles of progressive exposure, but it's your call to make.

2. You conduct all the activities.

Have a clear agreement that the support person will not take over any key functions. For instance, if you're doing driving exposure, you do all the driving. If you go for driving exposure with the idea that your support person can be an alternate driver, it lessens the chance that you will experience the anxiety, which is the whole point of the exposure exercise.

3. The support person doesn't tell you what to do, but offers reminders of what you planned to do.

The support person is there to bear witness to your efforts, to see things you don't notice because of your anxiety, and to offer reminders of your plan. The support person would helpfully say things like these:

- "I notice you're holding your breath. Do you want to do your breathing?"
- "Do you want to fill out a panic diary?"
- "I notice you suddenly got very quiet, are you having a panic attack?"
- "I know you're scared, that's good practice, hang in there."

4. *The support person doesn't try to protect you from the fear.*

Support people let you get the practice with panic that you need for recovery. They don't offer guarantees of your personal safety, promise to protect you from harm, or assure you there is nothing to be afraid of. Neither do they distract you in an effort to minimize your fear.

5. *Include the presence and absence of your support person in your hierarchy of exposure tasks.*

Once you are reasonably comfortable with a particular task accompanied by your support person, start doing it without that person. If it involves driving a particular stretch of road, drop your support person off at a convenient location and do your driving. Ride the elevator while he waits in the lobby. Shop while she waits in the parking lot, and so on. You need a support person who doesn't mind being dropped off somewhere to wait while you go practice. (Always remember to pick them up again before returning home.)

6. *Have a plan for phasing out your support person.*

This could be as simple as an agreement that you will work together for one month on a certain frequency, and then review your status in order to cut back on the support person's involvement as soon as possible.

7. *Make sure the support person knows that he or she is, in fact, your support person.*

I've seen instances in which people secretly used a friend or relative as a support person without saying so. They'd do this by inviting the person to accompany them to a number of places, and relying on their companionship without explaining the role they were playing. This is the purest case of the support person being a "billboard," but this is not a good practice. Aside from being somewhat deceitful and manipulative, it creates a steady state of tension about the availability of this person, and a continuing need to create white lies and other fictions, which usually make you more nervous.

If you are willing and able to start the exposure work described in Part Three without a support person, more power to you. You will save time and effort in the long run, because you won't have to rely on anyone else in the early stages, and you won't have to phase them out in the later stages. But many people just don't feel able to start on their own. If your only alternative is avoidance, then by all means, use the help of a support person. Just recognize that you will need to phase him or her out as soon as possible. Letting go of your support person will be an important step in your recovery.

When choosing a support person, you want someone who you know is reliable, and who has some time to spare, because you don't want someone canceling out when you're mentally prepared to go out and do some exposure work. You want someone who has your best interests at heart. You want someone who can be a good listener, hear what you are saying, and work with that instead of substituting their own judgment for yours. You want someone who will respect your confidentiality and maintain your privacy. Most of all, you want someone who has enough emotional distance from your troubles that he or she is content to let you work at your own pace. You don't want someone who is in a big hurry for you to get better, whether it's because they hate to see you suffer or because they're really tired of doing the grocery shopping.

It's often better to enlist a good friend as a support person, rather than a spouse. Spouses can be good support people if they can leave the rest of your relationship behind when you go out for exposure. But if your spouse can't do that, pick someone else (and explain it to your spouse so he or she doesn't feel left out). You might liken it to the way some parents—good parents—can't find the emotional distance necessary to teach their children to drive. That's why schools have driver education teachers.

9

....

Where Do Emotions Come From?

If you were having trouble with an appliance, you could get help from the manual that came with it. It would tell you basically how the item works, describe the kinds of problems and malfunctions that can occur, and suggest solutions.

Unfortunately, you and your emotions don't come with a manual. It would be a big help if you did. I remember one woman struggling to explain to a group meeting why she continued to get overwhelmed by panic attacks even though she knew that they weren't going to kill her or make her crazy. She rambled for a while, trying out different explanations, and finally hit upon one that fit pretty well. "My emotions just overrun my logic," she said.

This happens in a lot of anxiety disorders. People don't have such troubles because they're stupid, misinformed, weak, or looking for excuses. It's just that their emotions overrun their logic.

It happens to millions of people, with all kinds of fears, phobias, worries, obsessions, and other anxiety problems. They get afraid. They think that's really bad—probably ominous or dangerous in some way—and they resist it. They try to talk themselves out of the fear, suppress it, or get rid of it somehow. This leads them to feel more afraid and keeps ratcheting upward, nervousness leading to more nervousness, until it seems out of control.

It isn't, of course, it just feels that way. We explored this in Chapter 3, when you reviewed what has actually happened to you as a result of a panic attack. The bottom line is that you get afraid, and then you get afraid of being afraid, and you keep getting more afraid until, for whatever reason, that particular episode ends. Then you go back to whatever you were doing—until the next time.

People can become severely hampered, even disabled by fears that they themselves recognize are unrealistic. The great majority of people who fear flying because they think their plane will crash acknowledge that, statistically, commercial aviation is the safest method of travel. But knowing that doesn't rid them of their fear.

People who get terrified when they stand up to make a presentation typically know the audience isn't going to hurt them or hate them, but they get afraid all the same. It's pretty much the same thing for people who are afraid of elevators or suffer from other phobias. People who are terrified of vomiting know that it's a common occurrence and that the survival rate for vomiting is virtually 100 percent, but that knowledge doesn't remove their fear. In extreme cases, people have even been known to fear that their head will explode, or that their mind will somehow get detached from their body and never find its way back. These fears persist even though the phobia sufferers realize full well that they aren't really going to happen. Simply understanding that the fears are unrealistic doesn't end them. In fact, it often leads people to feel more agitated, because they think they "should know better" and so they get upset with themselves—for feeling upset. They try even harder to get rid of the fears, and that effort makes them more afraid too.

This circular process is enough to make your head spin.

Understanding how emotions work makes it easier to respond in ways that calm you down instead of getting you more upset. In this way, you can develop a "users manual" for your emotions.

Where do emotions come from? What produces the specific emotions you experience?

Most people assume the answer is that events cause emotions—that if something good happens to you, you feel good, and if something bad happens, you feel bad. According to this common belief, emotions are literally something the world throws at you. But if that were true, we would all be powerless to influence our emotions. We would have to look to others, and to outside events, for the changes that would make us feel better. We'd have to somehow get the world to throw only good things our way. Viewing emotions as something beyond our control that just happens to us, like the weather, makes a person feel more helpless. Moreover, there's good reason to believe it's not really true.

Suppose you were in a class and took an exam on which everyone received the same grade—a *B*. **What would you predict about the emotional reactions of the students?**

❑ Everyone would have the same emotional reaction.

❑ Different people would have different emotional reactions.

Different people would have different reactions, wouldn't they? **Now, why do you suppose people have different reactions to the same event?**

_____

_____

_____

_____

If you answered that people's reactions depend on "what they think" about an event, in this case the meaning each person gives to the grade of B—you're on the right track. People who thought of themselves as C students (or worse) would consider a B a pretty good grade and be happy. Perfectionists who thought anything less than an A was inadequate would be unhappy.

Here's another example, one that illustrates how thoroughly this mistaken idea about emotions permeates our culture and language. When someone tells you about their visit to a comedy club, they will often say of the comedian, "He made me laugh." But have you ever noticed that with most jokes, only some of the people laugh? Why doesn't the comedian "make" _all_ of them laugh? Wouldn't he get on the _Tonight Show_ sooner that way? The fact is, he doesn't actually _make_ anybody do anything. He tells a joke, but it's the people in the audience who give it meaning. Whether they laugh or not depends on the meaning they give it.

If somebody throws a bucket of water at me, and his aim is good, I get wet—regardless of what I think about it. That's a purely physical result of something the external world does to me. But if somebody throws an insult at me, the result is not nearly so automatic. My reaction depends on what I tell myself the insult means.

Consider the following scenarios in which you might receive an insult. Would you expect the same emotional reaction to each one, or different reactions?

- Your best friend calls you a slob.
- A panhandler on the street calls you a slob.
- A tourist calls you a slob in German.
- An actor reads this line from a script: "You are a slob."
- A comedian calls you a slob.
- Your mother calls you a slob.
- My mother calls you a slob.
- Your two-year-old son calls you a slob.

See what I mean? Your reaction is heavily influenced by what you tell yourself it means. A bucket of water tossed at you means you get wet, period. But

An Emotion Manual

If we had a manual for our emotions, it would include these central points:

1) Our thoughts shape the emotions we experience.

The meaning we give to events—the way we think of various events as good or bad—influences our emotions.

2) No matter whether our thoughts are true or false, they will still shape our emotions.

It doesn't matter how true or untrue our thoughts are; they shape our emotions all the same. For instance, if a bank teller dropped a book out of your field of vision, making a sudden sharp noise, you might assume it was a gunshot and feel afraid. However, if you actually saw him drop the book, you'd know it was harmless and wouldn't have a strong emotional reaction. Whatever you believed would shape and color your emotional response.

3) Our emotions are influenced by thoughts even, or perhaps especially, when we're not paying attention to those thoughts.

One reason people think that emotions are caused by external events is that they may not notice or remember the thoughts that preceded them. When I ask people what they were thinking just before a panic attack or an angry outburst, their first reply is often that they weren't thinking anything—that the emotions and physical sensations just came over them "out of the blue." It seems that way, because the emotion they experienced was so powerful that it attracted all their attention and memory. When they review the situation objectively, people can usually recall subtle thoughts and images that preceded the emotion.

The truth is, we're always thinking. There's hardly ever a time when we're "not thinking anything," even when we're asleep. We don't always pay attention to what we're thinking—or even notice that we *are* thinking…but we are.

4) We can become unconsciously repetitive and "stuck" in our thoughts, causing us to become "stuck" in emotional cycles.

There is reason to believe that thoughts are like other habits—that once we fall into a particular way of thinking, we tend to stay with it, thinking automatically without taking time to review or question the validity of our thoughts.

5) Opposing phobic thoughts often gives them more energy. Deliberate exposure to those thoughts deprives them of energy.

The more you try to protect yourself from your scary thoughts, the more your emotions will override your logic. If instead you accept scary thoughts and work with them, you'll find that you recover from them more quickly.

when an insult is tossed at you, your reaction depends on what you think about the insult, the person saying it, the context, and so on.

In short, most emotions are largely shaped by our thoughts. They are reactions to what we tell ourselves is happening, much more than to what is actually happening.

All this suggests that we play a role in the emotions we experience, that we aren't simply passive recipients of the emotions we feel. Our thoughts have a powerful influence on our emotions. Therefore, when we're not getting the emotions we want, it makes sense to take a closer look at our thoughts.

That's the "cognitive" part of the cognitive behavioral approach to treating panic attacks, which we'll be discussing in detail farther along in this book.

There's one more key point. Thoughts have a powerful mystique. We tend to view thinking as an activity that separates us from the rest of the animal kingdom, that our ability to think is the product of billions of years of evolution, the best and noblest product of God and the universe.

And, of course, each of us tends to think that our own thoughts are particularly good. Unless we have a particular reason to think about them, we tend to automatically assume that our thoughts are all true, useful descriptions of the world and our place in it. We know there's a good chance that our friends and relatives are mistaken in *their* thoughts, but we assume *ours* are highly accurate and valid.

This isn't a matter of pride. It's just as true for people who think of themselves as having low self-esteem as it is for those who consider their self-esteem to be high. Although pride of authorship is a contributing factor, our belief in the correctness of our own thoughts has more to do with the automatic, unconscious way in which we think.

Exploring the Emotional Impact of Thoughts

Let's look at another aspect of troublesome thoughts by conducting an experiment. Take the scariest thought you experience during a panic attack and put it into a one-sentence question that combines your initial "what if" fear with a description of the catastrophic outcome you fear will be the result. Here are few examples:

- What if I put some food in my mouth, choke on it, and die?
- What if I get trapped in the elevator all weekend and scream until I go insane?
- What if I panic in the restaurant, give myself an aneurysm, and become a vegetable?
- What if I drive off the bridge, get trapped underwater, and slowly asphyxiate?
- What if I freak out at the party, have a nervous breakdown, and spend the rest of my life in the hospital?

Now write one of your own:

_____

_____

_____

_____

_____

_____

Okay, now say your fear, slowly, out loud, 35 times. There's a sound thera-peutic reason for this, so do it right now, before you have time to talk your-self out of it. Don't stop—do all 35.
What did you observe? Any surprises?

_____

_____

_____

_____

How did the last repetition compare with the first one in terms of its emo-tional effect on you? Did you find that the last one had less emotional impact than the first one?

_____

_____

_____

If you observed that your thought lost some emotional "punch" as you repeated it over and over, then you've just discovered a new way to help yourself cope with thoughts that cause panic attacks. Instead of trying to get the thought out of your mind somehow like by arguing with it or distracting yourself—go ahead and repeat the thought out loud.

If you recognize this experiment for what it is—practicing _exposure_ to an unpleasant thought—it makes a lot of sense. This repetition is what's called a _desensitization procedure._ The thought becomes less disturbing the more times you repeat it because you're desensitizing yourself to it. Isn't this better than trying to keep the thought _out_ of your mind—and further sensitizing yourself to it?

10

....

The Rule of Opposites

Here's a rule you will probably find very helpful:

*When you experience a panic attack, become
consciously aware of your gut reaction—and do the opposite.*

That's not a misprint.

It may sound radical or bizarre, like some runaway version of reverse psychology. But the Rule of Opposites is a powerful and helpful response to the panic trick.

As we've seen, panic fills you with powerful sensations that fool you into thinking that you're in danger. You develop the proverbial "fear of fear" and try to protect yourself from fear. This makes your condition worse. Phobias aren't produced by a disease, a chemical imbalance, or some terrible disorder that attacks you. Phobias are the result of excessive self-protection.

They're the result of following your gut instinct to protect yourself from the fear. This instinct systematically gives you the wrong advice when you panic. It tells you to fight, to flee, to resist and to struggle. That would help if the problem were *danger*. But when the problem is *discomfort*, it only makes things worse.

Imagine that you're lost in the forest with a broken compass, one that always points south instead of north. Wait—don't throw it away! You can still use that compass to find your way home. You just have to remember to go the opposite direction from the one the compass indicates.

In the same way, even if your gut instinct is giving you the wrong advice, you can still use it as a guide during a panic attack. You just have to turn it around and do the opposite of what it demands.

The panic trick is diabolical. It tricks you into responding in exactly the way that will make the panic stronger and more persistent. It's practically the perfect crime. Even as you get tricked, you think you're saving yourself somehow. This is what people refer to when they say things like "I know I make it worse" or "I'm my own worst enemy."

The Rule of Opposites offers you a way to undo the trick.

The Opposite of Panic

Take a few minutes to consider how following the Rule of Opposites would change your typical response to a major panic attack. Most people, when they have a panic attack, do a number of things almost automatically. They hold their breath, tense their leg muscles, back, and jaw, hunch up their shoulders, look frantically for an exit, and try to hide their fear.

What do you usually do? Make a list of your automatic responses. For each one, write down how those responses affect you.

RESPONSES	EFFECT
_____	_____
_____	_____
_____	_____
_____	_____
_____	_____
_____	_____
_____	_____
_____	_____
_____	_____
_____	_____

What would be the opposite of each of your responses above, and how would each opposite response change the way you feel in the situation?

_____	_____
_____	_____
_____	_____

_____   _____

_____   _____

_____   _____

_____   _____

_____   _____

_____   _____

Fear on the Golden Gate Bridge

Here's an example from my own life that illustrates applying the Law of Opposites. I have a fear of heights in certain circumstances—very high, open places like tall cliffs, bridges, and rooftops. I'm only afraid when I'm out in the open. If I'm driving a car or looking out a window, it doesn't usually bother me. Living in Chicago most of my adult life, I rarely experienced those high, open situations. But occasionally, when I have the opportunity to visit San Francisco, I take a walk across the Golden Gate Bridge as part of my own personal work in exposing myself to heights.

I can get very afraid when I do this, even though the bridge is commonly used by people walking between Sausalito and San Francisco. One of the first times I tried it, I noticed that I was walking very slowly, with every muscle in my body strained tight. I was so afraid of losing my balance that I was practically scraping the soles of my shoes along the bridge surface, trying to walk without lifting my feet off the ground any more than was absolutely necessary.

I remembered the Rule of Opposites. At that moment, I really wished I hadn't remembered, because I knew right away what it was telling me. . . I was sorely tempted to ignore it and keep walking in the same tense way. But, considering my profession, I felt I had to taste my own medicine.

So I stood still for a moment—well away from the railing, of course—and then hopped up and down several times. I wasn't looking to jump off; I just wanted to do the opposite of holding my body so tensely.

And guess what? I immediately felt better. My body relaxed, and I started moving around a little more quickly (though grandmothers were still passing me). To stand there and hop—exactly the opposite of my gut instinct—really cut the tension and helped me feel better.

The Rule of Opposites will probably be a major help to you when you work on your own program of progressive exposure. For now, simply keep it in mind and plan on asking yourself these questions the next time you experience panic:

- Is it discomfort, or is it danger?
- What's my gut instinct right now?
- What's the opposite of that?

You don't even have to commit yourself to using this strategy. Just think about it and see what opposite responses it suggests to you next time you panic.

11

....

Belly Breathing

"I can't catch my breath!"

It's probably the most common of all the panic symptoms. Your breathing is short and shallow, you strain to get air, you fear you're not going to get it—and the harder you try, the worse it feels. But when your doctor, or the emergency room, gets your test results back, they tell you nothing's wrong.

There *is* something wrong, but it's not dangerous. What's wrong is that people who experience panic attacks tend to breathe in a way that actually *creates* many of the powerful physical symptoms of a panic attack. You've probably heard something like this before, but nobody ever really showed you how to correct it. I'm going to show you right now.

When first introduced to the subject of breathing, some panic attack sufferers are doubtful. It may be because simply thinking about their breathing makes them nervous. It may be because they just don't see how breathing can be so important and they think all breathing must be pretty much the same. Or they say they've already heard about diaphragmatic breathing and know they're doing it correctly. Occasionally, someone even feels insulted by the idea that their troubles can be attributed in any way to breathing and think that this minimizes the trouble they're having.

But, much more often than not, powerful results can come from retraining your breathing. If I could only spend ten minutes advising a client with panic, I would use that time to show them the breathing. That's how powerful it can be.

When you feel short of breath during—or just before—a panic attack, it doesn't mean you're not getting enough air. In fact, when people say "I can't catch my breath," it actually shows that they are getting air, because we talk by making air vibrate. If you're talking, you're breathing. Feeling short of breath is a common part of a panic attack, and it's not dangerous. You're getting enough air to live, but in an uncomfortable way that leads directly to sensations of panic. This happens when people breathe from their chest rather than their *belly*. It also happens when people hold their breath for long periods of time—something that people who talk very fast are prone to do—and when people hyperventilate.

Short, shallow chest breathing is very common among people with panic attacks, and it actually produces many of the other physical symptoms of a panic attack. Just about all the symptoms that trick you into thinking you're having a heart attack are the result of this kind of breathing:

- *Chest Pain*—When you breathe with your chest muscles, rather than your belly, the chest muscles can get so tight and tense that they hurt. Those are your chest muscles, not your heart muscle, that hurts.
- *Feeling Lightheaded or Dizzy*—Sensations that may result from the overbreathing (described in Chapter 4).
- *Numbness or Tingling in the Extremities*—Another temporary, harmless byproduct of the overbreathing.
- *Increased Heart Rate*—The increase is typically quite small and doesn't bring your heart rate nearly as high as the recommended heart rate for such cardiovascular exercise as running, bicycling, or swimming.

So here you are, lightheaded, feeling like you can't catch your breath, noticing an increased heart rate, pain in your chest and numbness in your left arm. No wonder you think you're having a heart attack.

It's a trick, and a very good one. All those symptoms certainly seem like a heart attack. But they're all produced by the short, shallow breathing, and they're harmless, uncomfortable, not dangerous. With belly breathing, you'll be able to bring these symptoms to an end. This will be a major step in your recovery.

You've probably already heard from other sources that what you need to do is "take a deep breath." If you're like most people, that advice hasn't helped you much. It's correct, but it's incomplete. It doesn't tell you *how* to take a deep breath, and it leaves out a very important detail.

The Way You Breathe Now

Imagine that you've come to my office for a consultation about your panic attacks. We're talking about the shortness of breath you experience during a panic attack, and probably other symptoms associated with breathing.

I ask you what you did in an effort to get your breath back.

You say you "took a deep breath."

I ask you to show me.

This simple request presents a valuable opportunity to learn about breathing and panic, so go ahead and **imitate what you did to take a deep breath when you felt short of air.**

Go ahead. Try it right now. (It's okay, nobody's watching.)

Take three deep breaths. Observe carefully how you do it. Then answer the following questions:

What was the first thing you did to take a deep breath?

_____

If you're like most people, you *inhaled*.

What muscles, in what part of your body, did you use to breathe?

_____

If you're like most people, you used your *upper body*. Even though you've been reading about belly breathing since the beginning of this chapter, chances are you used your chest and shoulders, and the motion of your breathing was probably up and down, as if you were lifting your upper body toward the ceiling.

And how did it feel? Comfortable?

_____

If you're like most people, your answer is "no."

Before I show you how to do belly breathing for real, let me remind you about the Rule of Opposites: when you start to panic, it will help to notice your gut reaction—and do the opposite.

What's the opposite of the "deep breath" you just took?

_____

This is an odd question, and people often have trouble with it. If you're one of them, move on to the following question:

Imagine that we took some video of you taking your "deep breath," and then ran the videotape backward. What would it look like?

_____

_____

_____

_____

Do you see what I mean? The opposite of what most people do when they try to take a deep breath is an *exhale*, the relaxing part of the breath. When you've been breathing from your chest, and those muscles are tight, you need a good relaxing exhale before you can switch to belly breathing. Before you can take a deep breath, you have to give one away.

The first thing most people do, when they're trying to "get their breath back," is inhale. But it doesn't give them the relief they want. When a person who has been breathing in a short, shallow manner immediately tries to take a deep inhale, they don't get a deep breath. All they get is another labored, shallow breath from the chest. It gives them all the air they need, but it doesn't feel good. The harder someone tries, the more tightness (rather than air) they get.

Exercise: Belly Breathing

Now let's practice belly breathing. You used to do it all the time. In fact, everybody does it when they're born. Stop in and visit the newborns in any maternity ward, and you'll see some world-class belly breathers. Their little bellies go out when they inhale and in when they exhale. Their upper body doesn't do the work, their bellies do. Nobody's told them yet to hold their stomachs in.

You used to breathe that way when you were a child. At some point, probably when you were a teenager, you shifted to chest breathing. Maybe you started paying attention to your body and felt you'd look more attractive if you held your stomach in. Maybe your mom corrected your posture and told you "stomach in, chest out." Whatever the reason, once you started holding your stomach in, you began breathing with your upper body, because there wasn't anything else to use.

Now is a good time to get back to belly breathing. Here's how.

1. Place one hand so it straddles your belt line and the other on your chest, right over the breastbone. You can use your hands as a simple biofeedback device. They will tell you what part of your body, and what muscles, you are using to breathe.

2. Open your mouth and sigh as if someone had just told you something really annoying. As you do, let your shoulders and the muscles of your upper body relax downward with the exhalation. The point of the sigh is not to completely empty your lungs—but to relax the muscles of your upper body.

3. Pause for a few seconds.

4. Close your mouth. Inhale slowly through your nose by pushing your stomach out. That's right, push your belly out, just like newborn infants do. This isn't a beauty contest. The movement of your stomach precedes the inhalation by just the tiniest frac-

tion of a second, because this motion pulls the air in. When you've inhaled as much air as you comfortably can (without throwing your upper body into it), just stop. You're finished with that inhale.

5. Pause briefly. How long? You decide. Everybody has different size lungs and counts at a different rate. Pause for whatever time feels comfortable, and be aware that when you breathe this way, you are taking larger breaths than you're used to. For this reason, you should *breathe more slowly* than you are used to. It's probably necessary to breathe even more slowly than seems reasonable at first. If you breathe at the same rate you use with small, shallow breaths, you will probably get a little lightheaded from overbreathing. It's not harmful. Lightheadedness and yawning are simply signals to slow down. Follow them.

6. Open your mouth. Exhale through your mouth by pulling your stomach in.

7. Pause.

8. Close your mouth and go back to the inhale.

9. Continue for a few minutes until you feel satisfied.

Let your hands be your guide. They will tell you whether you're doing it correctly or not. Where is the muscular movement of the breathing? You want it to occur at your stomach; your upper body should be relatively still. If you feel movement in your chest, or notice your head and shoulders moving upward, start again at Step 1 and practice getting the motion down to your stomach.

If you're doing it properly, you will feel a more comfortable effect very quickly.

Go ahead, spend a few minutes experimenting with belly breathing right now. Play around with it, but don't try to perfect it yet.

If you're like most people with panic, this is probably the *opposite* of how you've been breathing. It's the Rule of Opposites at work. Belly breathing may feel awkward at first, because there isn't another habit in your entire life that you've repeated more often than breathing. Don't let that bother you. It just means you need persistent, patient practice. Here are some troubleshooting tips to help you past the usual difficulties:

• If you have trouble redirecting your breathing from your chest to your stomach, practice isolating your stomach muscles first. Practice pushing your stomach out, then in, without breathing. As you get good at that, begin to pair it with your breathing.

• Practice in a variety of postures. When you're sitting down, you may find that either leaning back in the chair, or leaning forward with your forearms on your thighs makes it a little easier than sitting perfectly straight.

- Practice lying on your back. You can put something moderately heavy, like a big dictionary or city phone book, on your chest to make it easier to focus on using your stomach muscles.

- Practice lying on your front with a pillow beneath your stomach.

- Practice in front of a full length mirror, to see what you are doing.

- If you are unable to breath comfortably through your nose, because of allergies or some other reason, you can inhale through your mouth, but you have to inhale even more slowly to avoid gasping and gulping your air.

- Get rid of the gum. It makes you inhale with your mouth rather than your nose.

Once you can do this comfortably, get into the habit throughout your waking day of practicing every hour on the hour. At one o'clock, two o'clock, and so on, briefly notice how you're breathing. Then sigh, gently exhale, and continue with your belly breathing for a minute or so.

Don't interrupt your activity, just fit the breathing into whatever you're doing at the moment. If you did all your breathing practice in a comfy chair, after a while that would be the only place you could breathe comfortably. The goal here is to have frequent, brief practice sessions, shifting to comfortable belly breathing in a variety of activities, locations, and postures.

Besides hourly practice, here's another habit to cultivate. Whenever you notice that you're experiencing any kind of discomfort, be it anger, fear, worry, a headache, or a backache, sigh and shift into belly breathing for a few minutes. This way you'll develop the habit of making the shift whenever you're uncomfortable, and that's a great habit to have.

Do this as well. The day after you start your hourly breathing practice, stop and review how frequently you remember to actually do it. If you're doing it at least 75 percent of the time, good, keep it up for a week or two. If you're not that consistent, find something to remind you on a regular basis. Tie a string around your finger; wear your watch on the opposite hand or practice each time a frequent, routine event occurs, such as an office telephone ringing.

It may sound like a lot, practicing every hour. But after all, you're going to be breathing anyway. A week or so of this practice can really make a lasting difference in how you breathe.

Do you have to breathe this way all the time? The answer is no. Just focus on mastering the technique through regular, brief practice. Then use it when you have a panic attack. Over time, you'll find that you use this kind of breathing more and more as you make it your new habit. It happens naturally when you practice the suggestions above.

If you feel self-conscious about belly breathing, or worry that this unusual activity may bring unwanted attention your way, try to notice how other people breathe. You'll find that there's quite a bit of variety in breathing habits—and nobody cares.

To view a video clip in which I demonstrate this technique, visit my website at www.anxietycoach.com.

12

....

Self-Hypnosis

Here's a simple, self-hypnotic exercise you can use whenever you want to take a few minutes to relax. You may want to make it a habit, doing it routinely once or twice a day for your own comfort (think of it as "mental floss"). You can also use it when you're experiencing high anxiety or panic—maybe on an airplane, riding as a passenger in a car, or during a long wait at a doctor's office. It's amazing how much benefit you can get from such a simple method.

Hypnosis is a technique based on mental focus and breathing, as are other relaxation techniques such as yoga, guided imagery, and meditation. Hypnosis allows you to relax by focusing your attention more and more narrowly, perhaps on a single word, sound, picture, or sensation. This allows you to quiet the internal chatter of your mind and relax your body as well.

There's a lot of mystique, myth, and misunderstanding about hypnosis, which leads some people to fear it, but it's really a simple, natural experience—the same kind of experience you might have while watching a really good movie, responding emotionally, intellectually, and physically as if it were actually happening to you or other people you care about. You can become so involved in a film that you don't seem to notice the ordinary sights, sounds, and smells around you. Other people, the smell of popcorn, the exit signs seem to fade out of your consciousness, yet when the movie ends, you get up and go about your business as before.

The hypnotic experience is similar—it's not something a hypnotherapist "causes" to happen, nor is it a form of "mind control." Rather, it's something the hypnotic subject (that's you, if you want to be) *allows* to happen. Contrary to popular myth, a person in hypnosis can remember as much of the experience as he wants and cannot be compelled to do anything against his or her will. Of course, when you do self-hypnosis, you can feel even more confident that you are in charge, because no one else is involved.

Research has shown that people with panic and anxiety disorders have more than the average amount of hypnotic ability and thus are good candidates to use hypnosis if they choose to do so. A panic attack, as we've seen, is actually a "what if" experience in which you think and feel the way you would if something terrible were actually happening. Panic taps into your imagination, your ability to think and feel "as if."

That's what hypnosis does, too. It uses the same abilities that make you susceptible to panic attacks, but it does so in a healthy way. "What if . . . I were relaxing on a sunny beach, drifting in and out of a peaceful sleep, hearing the ocean waves and the sea birds in the background. . ."

Exercise: Hypnotizing Yourself

There are many different ways of doing self-hypnosis. The method I describe here is about as simple and straightforward a method as you're likely to find.

Here are a few guidelines to enhance your experience in using this method—and one requirement.

First, the requirement. Since this is a relaxation technique, practice this only in situations where you are truly free to relax, with no important responsibilities or safety issues requiring your attention. Don't use this technique while operating any kind of machinery, including cars and other vehicles.

And now for the guidelines:

- Don't "try hard" at doing this. Don't try at all. Trying will just get in your way. Simply follow the steps listed below, allowing whatever happens to happen.

- For your first few experiences, practice in a quiet, comfortable setting where you will not be disturbed by others, the telephone, your pets, or whatever.

- If you wear hard contact lenses, remove them (in case you fall asleep). Remove or loosen any constrictive clothing. If you like, use a fan, aquarium, or white noise machine to provide ongoing, repetitive background sound.

- Don't evaluate how you're doing or be concerned with how much or little relaxation you experience. Simply allow yourself to go through the steps, and save the judgments for later.

- Relaxation is like sleeping or enjoying a good meal. It doesn't make sense to try to "make" yourself sleep or to try harder to get enjoyment from your food. You simply create the right circumstances and allow the sleep or the flavor to come. Follow the same process to let yourself relax.

- You can do self-hypnosis with your eyes open or closed.

Pick Your Own Cue Word

A cue word is simply a one-syllable word you use to focus your attention. It doesn't matter what the word is, so long as it's fairly neutral. I wouldn't use words such as "kill" or "sex." In my personal practice, I use the word "small." If you can't think of a word to use, you can use my word or any one-syllable word like "one," "calm," or "now."

- You can depart from the steps listed below. If you forget what number you were on, do a step out of order, or forget a step altogether, don't be concerned. This is not a recipe; it is a process for relaxation that will not suffer if you change it.
- You don't have to memorize these steps before you begin. It's enough to read them through once or twice and then refer back to them for guidance as you proceed.
- Finally, you can do this with a desire to get as deeply relaxed as possible; or you can do this just out of curiosity, to see what it's like. Come as you are.

As you become more familiar and comfortable with this method, you can begin to use it in a variety of settings. It's not necessary to limit yourself to a quiet place. You can do this on an airplane, or standing in line, or a variety of other locations. The suggestion of a quiet, comfortable place is just to make it easier to get started. I've had occasion to use this in an MRI machine, a particularly noisy and uncomfortable situation.

The Steps

1. Begin by sitting comfortably (or lying down, if you prefer; in that case, elevate your head slightly with a pillow). Sigh gently and use that exhalation to relax your shoulders and upper body. Do your belly breathing for a few moments.

2. As you feel your breathing relax, begin to focus on a cue word, repeating it silently and slowly on each exhale.

3. After a few moments of focusing on the cue word (maybe 6 to 12 repetitions, but the number isn't important), stop repeating the word and make the following suggestion to yourself: "I'm going to let myself relax now." Simply say or think those words to yourself in a permissive way, without commanding or demanding anything.

4. Continue your belly breathing, count down silently and slowly on each exhale, from 20 to 15.

5. At 15 or thereabouts, pause to give yourself another gentle suggestion. You might choose to simply repeat the first one. If you have any special reason for this particular relaxation, you could state it now, for example, "I'm going to let myself float through these panicky feelings." Use only positive, permissive suggestions. Avoid any suggestions that urge you to make any kind of effort, to achieve a particular goal, or to stop doing something. (Examples of unhelpful suggestions would be: "I'm going to try to relax more than ever before" and "I *have* to stop worrying about the stock market right now!")

6. Resume counting down on the exhales, from 14 to 10 or so.

7. At the count of 10 or thereabouts, stop counting. If you're doing this exercise with your eyes closed, open them now, look briefly to your right and your left, then close your eyes again if you wish, and go back to Step 1, repeating the entire sequence again. (Or, if you're doing it with your eyes open, blink slowly several times, look briefly to your right and your left, and go back to Step 1, repeating the entire sequence again.)

8. Go through the entire sequence three times.

9. After the third time, give yourself a final suggestion, something that fits your circumstances. If you're ready to go to sleep, say something about sleeping comfortably. Or you can give yourself a suggestion about the rest of your day—something like: "Now I'm going to return my attention to the present, returning with an alert, focused mind in a more comfortable state, looking forward to the activities of the rest of my day."

This is a very brief exercise—it usually take less than five minutes, sometimes only one or two. Experiment with it frequently.

13

....

Control

People with panic attacks and phobias worry a lot about control. They often fear that they are going to "lose control" of themselves and act in a bizarre or dangerous way that will ruin their life. They tend to expect that they should be able to "control" their thoughts and emotions, experiencing only the ones they want to have. "After all," the reasoning goes, "it's my mind, and I should be in control of it, right?"

Well, wrong, actually.

The truth is, you don't control your mind. You can't have only the thoughts or emotions you want. While you can influence the way your mind works, by working with thoughts and emotions in the way we discussed in Chapter 9, you can't have absolute control. In fact, the harder you try to prevent particular thoughts and emotions, the more likely you are to experience them. You'll almost always get better results by working *with* the thoughts and emotions that come up instead of trying to order up the thoughts and emotions you want.

So start by asking yourself, how do we actually measure control? In our society, what yardstick do we use to conclude whether a person is "in control" or not? Write your thoughts here.

_____

_____

_____

_____

_____

_____

_____

Control is measured by behavior—by what people actually do, not by what they feel or think. As long as your behavior fits what is expected for your particular role, you're regarded as being in control of yourself.

When I say "role," I mean the part you play in whatever setting or activity you're in. If, as a tennis player, you start punching your opponent, you're out of control. If as a boxer, you do the same thing, you're not. If, as a passenger on a commercial jet, you insist on talking to the pilot about the appropriate speed and altitude of the plane, you're out of control. If you do so as a co-pilot, you're not.

People with panic attacks worry because they have thoughts such as "What if, when I panic, I drive off the bridge?" or "What if I try kicking out the window on the airplane?" They assume that, because they think it, they're liable to do it.

Are your thoughts and emotions a good predictor of your behavior?

Not really, no.

A much better predictor of what you're likely to do in the future is what you've done in the past.

Do you fear losing control of yourself during a panic attack? If so, describe your fear fully here. What do you fear you will do, and what do you fear will be the result?

_____

_____

_____

_____

_____

Now, review your personal history very carefully. What is the worst thing—the most out-of-control thing—you've ever done in response to such fears?

_____

_____

_____

_____

_____

If you have an actual history of "acting out" in some antisocial or unacceptable way, you need to address that issue with the help of a psychologist or other therapist skilled in working with such problems. But if all you have is the fear, and not the history of actual misbehavior, then it would be a reasonable approach to treat these fears of losing control as simply another "what if" thought that only means "I'm afraid."

Control Issues and Phobias

Concerns about control influence all phobias. Let's take a look at how they influence two particular phobias: the fears of flying and public speaking. On the surface, the two may not seem to have much in common, but in actuality they both reflect the same fundamental problem—the one that develops when you don't accept the role you happen to be in at any given time and the degree of control that comes with it.

Each of these activities, flying and public speaking, offers you a certain *role* to play. People who accept the offer and play the role increase their comfort level with the activity and circumstances. People who resist the role, and try to have it another way, decrease their comfort level with the activity and circumstances.

The Fear of Flying

If you fly somewhere on a commercial airline, your role is that of a *passenger*. As such, you control nothing about the airplane, and you may know very little about its operation. There is a professional crew whose job it is to handle the airplane and all tasks associated with it. They work together with other professionals on the ground to control the aircraft, including such factors as when you can board, when the door closes, when the plane takes off, when you can move about the cabin and use the bathroom, when you get your snack or beverage, what information you receive from the cockpit or the flight attendants, and when you get to your destination.

As a passenger, you are "baggage that breathes." You control no aspect of the flight, nor do you have any particular influence over how the flight operates— whether it's on time or late, smooth or turbulent, quiet or noisy, safe or unsafe, and so on. The role of a passenger is simply to show up and pass the time as comfortably as possible while waiting for the vehicle to arrive at its destination. As far as passengers are concerned, a jetliner is a waiting room in the sky.

People who fear flying hate this. They don't want to be just a passenger; instead, they want to think they have some control over what happens. They may even try to act as if they're part of the crew. For instance, a lot of fearful fliers don't want other people to talk to them during takeoff. They think they have to pay attention to the takeoff, listen to the engines, and watch the angle of flight. They don't want to be distracted from "their job."

Other fearful fliers will monitor the Weather Channel for a week or more before their flight, as if they will be called upon for their opinion about whether or not it's safe for the airplane to fly that day. As a passenger, you can be quite sure the FAA will not be involving you in this decision. They already have experts on the payroll for that.

People who fear flying tend to resist the role of passenger, striving to create the illusion of control over the situation any way they can. This struggle for control when it's out of your hands is a big factor in producing and maintaining the fear of flying.

The Fear of Public Speaking

If you agree to make a presentation to a group, however reluctantly, you agree to take on the role of *speaker*. The purpose of that role is to give relevant material to an audience, directing their attention to what you have to say and generally controlling the agenda. The audience relinquishes a lot of power to a speaker. The speaker controls his presentation of the material—the order, pacing, content, and so on—while the audience agrees to sit down, be quiet, and listen. If the speaker asks the audience a question, they will respond, whether aloud or in their minds. The speaker can poll the audience about an issue, and they will raise their hands. If it's a long presentation, the speaker can decide when to let the audience take a bathroom break, when to allow refreshments, and when to invite them to ask questions. In short, the speaker has the control.

People who fear public speaking hate this. They avoid the exercise of this control like the plague. Instead, they often choose to be *unspeakers*, avoiding all the powers the audience has delegated to them. They may try to make their presentation as boring as possible, perhaps reading it in a monotone voice, averting their eyes from the audience, rushing through it in the hope that the audience will not pay too much attention, and certainly that they will not ask any questions.

People who fear public speaking tend to resist the role of speaker and avoid using the powers the audience and the hosts have entrusted to them. Avoiding the control that has been delegated to you is a big part of what produces and maintains the fear of public speaking.

Mirror Images of Control

We'll look at other aspects of each of these fears in later chapters. For now, let's just consider the fact that these two fears are the mirror images of each other. The fearful flier struggles to have control that can't be his. The fearful speaker tries to avoid control that has been handed over to him. Overcoming either of these fears involves identifying and accepting the role the activity offers you.

Flying on a commercial jet offers you the role of *passenger*, in which you delegate full control to the crew, make yourself as comfortable as you can, and wait for the completion of the trip. Speaking to an audience offers you the role of *speaker*, in which you accept the powers the audience has delegated to you and direct their attention and energy to the information you have agreed to impart to them.

To fully accept and work within these or any other role lessens the anxiety one feels. To resist and struggle against a role increases the anxiety one feels. This is the case, not just with these two particular fears, but with other phobias as well. For instance, concern about control is common among people who fear highway driving and are particularly fearful of entering the highway and merging with existing traffic. Merging involves giving other drivers a clear signal of your intentions. As you approach the point of merger, it's part of your role to clearly indicate, by your speed and your turn signals, whether you intend to enter in front of or behind them. Fearful drivers often want to avoid that part of their job and wait for the other drivers to make the choice for them. Avoiding the job creates more uncertainty and more, not less, anxiety.

Take a few minutes to think about your particular phobia. What is the natural role, or "job title," that comes with your phobic situation?_____

_____

In that role, what do people normally have to accept, and what do they normally control?

ACCEPT	CONTROL
_____	_____
_____	_____
_____	_____
_____	_____
_____	_____
_____	_____
_____	_____
_____	_____

In what ways do you create additional anxiety for yourself by trying to control what you can't, or by avoiding the control that is yours in that situation?

_____

_____

_____

_____

_____

How can you handle these aspects of your role differently?

_____

_____

_____

_____

_____

14

....

Progressive Exposure

Now the time has come to talk about the solution to panic and phobias: *progressive exposure.*

Many people, including some mental health professionals, misunderstand what exposure is all about. I can see why. It doesn't reflect common sense. In fact, as we saw with the Rule of Opposites, it defies common sense. What's more, the very idea of exposure can seem scary.

"Exposure" means practicing with panic. "Progressive" means doing it a step at a time, at a pace that is acceptable to you. You can go as slow as you need to or as fast as you're willing to.

To practice with panic, you need to create the right circumstances—the situations, activities, locations, and cues that usually provoke a panic attack in you.

If you tend to panic while driving on highways, your exposure program will emphasize highway driving. Ditto for shopping malls, elevators, supermarket lines, meetings, and so on.

You also need to be aware of the subtle details that influence your fear and build them into your practice. For instance, if you panic on highways while driving in the middle lane, but not while in the right lane where proximity to the shoulder offers comfort, you'll need . . . you guessed it . . . practice driving in the middle lane.

If you panic in elevators unless you press your body against the wall, you'll need to practice standing erect, in the middle of the elevator. Over time, you'll have to account for all the self-protective methods you listed in Chapter 5. If necessary, you can phase them out gradually instead of dropping them all at once, but they have to go—and the sooner, the better.

People often mistakenly think that exposure means going to the feared situation and striving not to panic. But that's not exposure, that's struggling to protect yourself from the panic—fighting the panic—and it will cause you more trouble in the long run.

The goal of progressive exposure isn't simply to expose yourself to the highways, or the shopping malls, elevators, grocery stores, or parties. That's only a means to an end. What you fear about those places isn't the place itself. Nobody starts to panic in Home Depot because they're afraid of ant traps and duct tape. Nobody walks down the dog food aisle in the supermarket and freezes in horror at the site of Milk Bones. Nobody panics in church for fear of the collection basket or the kneeling bench.

People fear those situations because they think that being in the situation will somehow lead to a panic attack. So they try to protect themselves by avoiding the situation or only going there when they feel "protected" by a support person or object, a superstitious rule, or some other protective device.

It's your efforts to protect yourself from the panic that allow your troubles to continue. The goal of exposure is to bring on a panic attack so that you can practice responding in a more comfortable manner. When doing exposure, you go to places where your presence is likely to lead to a panic attack. When the attack comes, you can practice working with it in a way that calms it down instead of building it up.

By exposing yourself to the fear and practicing with it, rather than protecting yourself from it, you can desensitize yourself. This powerful recovery method will lead you to become less and less afraid of having a panic attack. Once you're no longer afraid of panic attacks, they tend to fade away.

Learning to Get Hit

Progressive exposure is often hard, scary work. It calls upon you to approach, rather than avoid, the panic.

Let's suppose you wanted to learn self-defense and to become reasonably confident in your ability to protect yourself physically. You could read books about self-defense, maybe even practice some moves and techniques on your own. You could watch videos or DVDs and look up self-defense on the Internet. But without practice or experience, no amount of reading, viewing, or solitary practice would give you confidence that you could defend yourself. You wouldn't know for sure whether you could remember what to do in a fight, much less execute the moves properly.

Sooner or later, if you really wanted to learn and become confident in your self-defense abilities, you would need to take a class. There, an instructor would show you how to display a physical presence that discourages would-be assailants, to maintain an awareness of your environment, to block punches and kicks, and to distract, confuse, hit, discourage, and evade an opponent.

And the instructor would also hit you. . .

With your permission, or course, lightly, with an open hand or a single finger. Without the experience of getting hit, it would be hard to respond to a real-life attack. By taking a self-defense class, you accept sparring with the instructor and your classmates as part of the learning process.

Practicing with Panic

The attitude and approach you need to learn self-defense are similar to those that will help you solve the problem of panic attacks and phobias. When you work with phobias and panic attacks, you first learn some techniques and develop some ways of responding to the fears and symptoms. Then you go out and practice with the fears and the symptoms.

The point of the practice is *not* to avoid having a panic attack in a situation you fear. That would be like going to a self-defense class just to watch from the sidelines and take notes but refusing to participate. The point of exposure is to experience the panic symptoms themselves—and then stay there and let them pass. That's how you can learn to handle them and develop confidence in your ability to do so. Take exposure a step at a time, at a pace that's acceptable to you.

If you find yourself thinking, "That's the opposite of what I would do," that's a good sign. The Rule of Opposites means learning to act differently in panic situations, so doing the opposite of what you "normally" would mean that you're headed in the direction of recovery. Each time you find yourself tempted to act in old, avoidant, self-protective ways, remember that those are the ways that have maintained your troubles. If they were going to fix things, you'd be finished already.

Much of this book so far has been devoted to showing you how you've been tricked into thinking and behaving in ways that maintain and strengthen your panic. The coming chapters will show you how you can use that understanding to foster your own recovery—how to work "with" panic so that you can move on to do exposures and how to cope with the anticipatory anxiety you may be experiencing even as you read these words.

PART THREE

DOING EXPOSURE

15
....

How to Handle a Panic Attack

By now you might be thinking, "Okay, I got the idea! Panic attacks aren't dangerous, they just trick me into thinking that. Fine, I guess that's why I'm still alive and sane, more or less. If I go out and practice with them, I'm supposed to gradually lose my fear, and that makes enough sense that I'm willing to consider it. But . . . if I'm successful with the exposure, I'll have a panic attack! *What do I do then?*"

And well you might ask.

If you could do absolutely nothing—if you could just hang out and experience the panic—it would scare you and then go away. If you were totally confident that panic is harmless, it would have all the drama of a sneeze. It would disrupt you momentarily, and then you would return your attention to whatever you were doing before.

But because it's hard to be that confident, because panic tricks you into believing otherwise, you get fooled into resisting and trying to protect yourself. Therein lies the trouble. When you resist, you make it worse. You need a way to experience panic without resistance.

Organizing your response is very helpful. It doesn't make you safe, because you're already safe. You need to organize your response so you won't get tricked into making it worse. This chapter reveals ways to help you cope with the panic and your reactions to it so you can hang out and let it pass.

Lest you make it harder than it has to be, let's be clear about one thing at the outset. The exposure process is *not* like learning to juggle bowling balls and chain saws, where you'd have to get really good, really fast. For our purposes, getting "good enough," taking the process a step at a time at your own pace, will be good enough.

Here's a five-step process I've adapted from the excellent book *Anxiety Disorders and Phobia: A Cognitive Perspective*. You can use this process to guide your responses during a panic attack, whether in your exposure practice (when panic is always a good thing, because you need the practice) or at other times.

As you read this, think about how it compares to what you usually do during a panic attack, and make some notes in each section before you go on to the next. You will probably find some significant differences between these steps and what you usually do. That's just what we're looking for. That's where you want to make changes.

You will probably want to fine-tune these steps to reflect your particular needs in whatever situation your panic occurs. For instance, you will have some different responses to an attack that occurs while you are driving on the freeway, than to an attack that occurs while you are attending a staff meeting, or shopping in a grocery store. Feel free to customize these five steps and make them your own.

The five steps are summed up by the acronym **AWARE**. They are:

Acknowledge & Accept
Wait & Watch
Actions (to make yourself more comfortable)
Repeat
End

Step One: Acknowledge & Accept

The first step is to acknowledge the present reality—namely, that you are having a panic attack or feel like you're about to have one—and resign yourself to that experience as best you can. Point out to yourself that you're afraid, and remember that, miserable as the experience is, it's okay to be afraid, and it's okay to have a panic attack.

When you start feeling panicky while doing exposure work, you may find yourself thinking, "Oh, *no*! What did I come here for?" When you hear that question, remind yourself that you came here specifically to practice with your fears. The answer to this question is, "*This*—the fear—*is what I came for*. This is good practice. It will help me get over the panic attacks."

Purposefully notice the signs and symptoms of the attack, and allow yourself to experience them with as little resistance as possible. Whenever you catch yourself struggling against the panic, give up the struggle.

When you go outside on a bitterly cold day, chances are you instinctively tighten up your muscles, as if that would make you warmer. It actually makes you feel colder, and if you know that, you can get into the habit of relaxing those muscles each time you catch yourself tensing up. You can do the same thing with your instinctive urge to resist anxiety. When you catch yourself resisting, let go of the resistance—again and again. That's how you develop a new habit.

You might easily get upset with yourself as you catch yourself in the act of resisting again and again, but don't be fooled. When you catch yourself, *it's a good thing*. You've been resisting all along. The difference is that now you've caught yourself in the act. Good! That's the only way you'll have a chance to change the habit.

Your aim is to experience the panic in the same resigned manner you would accept a lecture from an unreasonable boss who doesn't want to hear your point of view—and who definitely won't be supervising you for long, because you have other plans. For the moment, it's in your interest to passively go along with it, because getting into a fight doesn't help you in the least.

Your aim is not to ignore the panic or pretend it's not there. Rather, it is to become desensitized to your feelings of fear and panic. When you catch yourself pretending or struggling to distract yourself, bring your attention back to the panic so that you can become less sensitive to these feelings. In the same way, when you find yourself commanding yourself to "stop thinking about it!," back off and let yourself think about it.

The fact you are called upon to acknowledge is that *you are afraid*. You may think that you are in danger, but you can recognize such thoughts as a sign that you are afraid—just another symptom of fear, not a realistic appraisal of the situation. Whenever you hear yourself having thoughts about being in terrible danger, recognize them as some of the usual symptoms you experience during an attack, nothing more.

Remember that thoughts aren't always true or profound. Often they're just trash talk, symptoms expressed in words rather than sensations. You don't like them, but you can accept them the same way you can accept feeling lightheaded, or crying, or experiencing butterflies in your stomach.

Accept the fact that you are afraid at this moment. Don't fight the feeling, or ask God to take it away, or blame yourself or others. Accept that you are afraid in the same way you would accept a headache. You don't like having a headache, but you wouldn't bang your head against the wall to try and get rid of it, because that would only make it worse.

You know from the Rule of Opposites that your gut instinct will be to do things that will only make the situation worse. Notice that instinct and recognize it as a symptom. You don't have to follow your gut instinct. In fact, you can do the opposite of what it suggests. Do nothing to make the panic worse. Don't struggle against it. Don't try to protect yourself. Just say to yourself, "Let it come."

You may wonder, "How can I accept a panic attack?"

Accept it by:

- staying in place
- allowing yourself to feel whatever you feel, and
- letting time pass.

You can accept a panic attack by responding to it the same way that you would respond to a policeman who pulls you over for speeding. Imagine you were only going four miles over the speed limit. You have a car full of wedding presents, and you're all dressed up as the best man or maid of honor. You're late for the reception and in a hurry to get there. But the police officer doesn't care. You can argue with him—and be even more late to the reception. You can cuss him out—and maybe get charged with other offenses. Or you can resign yourself to what seems like unfair punishment, and go on about your business.

Once you've made your mind up to acknowledge and accept a panic attack, you can do a few things to help make yourself a little more comfortable, a little less terrified, while you're waiting for it to end.

What Makes It Acceptable?

The fact is, although a panic attack feels awful and fills you with dread, it is not dangerous. It will not kill you or make you crazy. If you were actually in danger, of course, you'd have to do something to protect yourself. If somebody pointed a gun at you, you'd have to run, hide, fight, yell, bribe, or beg, because the consequence of being shot would be so terrible that you'd have to do whatever you could to avoid it. But for most people, the only consequence of a panic attack is that they get scared. When you're having one, you're already experiencing the worst. It can only get better. All you have to do is wait it out, give it time to pass.

You accept the panic attack because the more you resist, the worse it gets. And the more you accept it, the sooner it leaves.

How does "Acknowledge & Accept" compare to what you usually do?

ACKNOWLEDGE & ACCEPT	WHAT I USUALLY DO
1. I acknowledge I'm afraid.	1. _____
2. I let myself be afraid.	2. _____
3. I resign myself to it.	3. _____
4. I catch myself resisting, and put myself back on course.	4. _____ _____

Step Two: Wait & Watch

You can know in advance that your instincts will be quite the opposite of "wait & watch." When you panic, you know your gut reaction will be to distract yourself and blindly flee the situation. You also know that won't help. So, even as you plan to "wait & watch," be wary of the urge to do the opposite. When that urge comes, just get yourself back on track without wasting time and energy criticizing yourself.

"Wait & watch" is a latter-day version of something you learned as a child (back when you were still a belly breather): "Count to ten before you get mad." Waiting and watching works the same way.

One hallmark of a panic attack is that it temporarily robs you of your ability to think, remember, and concentrate. Waiting and watching will buy you a little time to regain those abilities before you take any action. If you react before you have a chance to think straight, you may flee, struggle, or do something else that makes you feel worse. This is what people mean when they say things like "I know I'm doing it to myself."

Of course, you will have a powerful urge to leave the scene of a panic attack. That's only natural. Watch for that urge, so you won't be surprised by it. When you observe it, recognize that exit is an option and postpone that decision for a little bit. Don't tell yourself you *can't* leave—keep that option open so you don't feel trapped—but put off the decision about whether or not to leave. Stay in the situation for the time being.

You will make the best progress by staying in the situation until the panic attack has come and gone. You could bring the attack to an immediate end by leaving, but remember that practice with panic was the reason you came here to begin with. You desensitize yourself to the fear each time you come and wait it out. Choose long-term freedom, not immediate comfort. Use the occasion to observe how the panic works, and how you respond to it.

How does "Wait & Watch" compare to what you usually do?

WAIT & WATCH	WHAT I USUALLY DO
1. I watch for myself to react hastily, and go back to waiting.	1. _____ _____ _____
2. I acknowledge the urge to flee, but stay in place and postpone the decision, keeping my options open.	2. _____ _____ _____
3. I observe my reactions and take notes on my experience.	3. _____ _____

Step Three: Actions
(To Make Yourself More Comfortable)

Now that you've taken a little time to acknowledge and accept, and wait and watch, you're in a good position to take some actions to help yourself.

Those first two steps are very important. They help you recognize what's going on, and to remember what your job is, before you rush into action. If you jump right into action without going through the first two steps, you're likely to overreact and make the situation worse, so discipline yourself to do the steps in order.

When the time for action comes, remember that it's *not* your job to bring the panic attack to an end. That will happen no matter what you do. Whether you remember these steps and soothe yourself or fall for the trick and make the panic worse, the attack still ends. Your job is simply to make yourself a little more comfortable, if you can, while you occupy your current role, such as shopper, driver, walker, or speaker, and wait for the attack to end.

If you have a panic attack in the supermarket, your role is still that of the shopper, so keep pushing that cart around the store, involving yourself with buying groceries, while letting the attack peak and pass so you can get on with your business.

Ask the Right Questions

Most people automatically ask themselves a lot of "why" questions during a panic attack. "Why me?" "Why now?" "Why here?" These questions are more heckling than help. For the most part, you won't be able to answer them.

The right questions to ask are "What's happening now?" and "How shall I respond to it?" These questions will direct your attention and memory to the useful responses you can make. Your dialogue with yourself might go something like this:

"What's happening now?"

"I'm having trouble catching my breath, and I'm starting to panic."

"Why is this happening to me?"

"Oh, there I go again. I caught myself asking the 'why' questions. Let's get back to 'what' and 'how.'"

"All right, how should I respond to it?"

"I'll sigh and start the belly breathing."

Make Yourself Comfortable

There's an important distinction to be made between helping yourself feel a little more comfortable while waiting for the attack to end, and trying to end the attack. The first is helpful; the second is not. The first involves accepting the attack and being aware of it. The second involves resisting and opposing the attack. The key is to coexist with the attack instead of fighting it. Do things to make yourself a little more comfortable even as you observe the attack proceeding.

Whatever else you do, do belly breathing (see Chapter 11). Then talk to yourself (silently) about what is happening and what you need to do. For instance, you might ask yourself, "Is this discomfort or danger?" Other responses might include the following:

- "Fine, let's have an attack. It's a good chance to practice my coping techniques."
- "So what if I worry about 'what if?' I'll get afraid, then calm down again."
- "It's okay to be afraid."

About Those "What If" Thoughts

People don't panic in the present. They panic when they imagine something bad happening to them in the future or remember it happening in the past. That's why your panic attacks are almost always accompanied by some "what if" thought. The reason you have to say "what if" is because what you fear is not happening at that moment.

To counter "what if" thoughts, get involved in what is going on around you at that moment. When you catch yourself imagining the future, the past, or other situations, take a moment to notice that you're doing it, be glad you caught yourself, and then get involved in what's right around you at that moment. Get back into the activity you were engaged in prior to the attack and become involved with the people and objects around you. If you're in a store, shop: read labels, compare prices, walk around, ask questions, put items in your cart, return items to the shelf, etc. If you're driving, drive: change lanes, make small adjustments to your speed, turn on the radio or change the station. If you're in a meeting, or at lunch in a restaurant, get involved in what is going on around you, even if you feel like you have to force it: ask a question, make a comment, get some water.

Don't try to force yourself to "stop thinking about it." Instead, notice and accept the fact that you are having these scary thoughts. Remind yourself that it's okay to be afraid. Then bring your focus and energy back to your immediate surroundings. Allow the "what if" thoughts to run their course while you become involved with what is around you.

Relaxation and Exercise

Learn to identify and relax the parts of your body that get most tense during a panic attack. This usually involves the muscles of the jaw, chest, shoulders, and legs. Tense, then relax, these muscles one set at a time. Do not allow yourself to stand rigid, muscles tensed, holding your breath. That just makes you feel worse. Instead, work with your muscles and posture to regain a sense of control over your body. If you feel like you "can't move a muscle," start with just one finger.

If you lean against a wall or other surface for support, move away and stand the way you usually do. Stand on one foot, just to see that you can do it. Hop up and down. This will let you test the notions that you're fragile, have weak balance, or will collapse if you don't struggle to hold yourself together.

If you're in a situation where it would be appropriate to get some cardiovascular exercise, such as running, walking, climbing stairs, or dancing, go ahead and do this. It will help you burn off some of that adrenaline. (While such exercise is safe and beneficial for the great majority of people, ask your physician if it is okay for you, and if he or she says yes, do it despite any misgivings you may have).

Think Long-Term

With respect to all other coping responses, follow the golden rule: Choose your long-term freedom, not immediate comfort. Do nothing that will make you more dependent or avoidant in the long run. When you experience a panic attack, you usually have to choose between immediate comfort (fleeing or other forms of protection) and long-term confidence and freedom. Opt for the long-term benefit. This is about your life, not just the next ten minutes.

When you have to make immediate choices about how to respond to a panic attack, ask yourself, "How do I want to feel later today, about four hours from now, when I think back to how I handled this attack?" Because that—*not* your safety or sanity—is what's really at stake in the moment of a panic attack. Will you feel pleased with yourself because you worked hard to treat panic like the sneaky trick it is, or feel disappointed in yourself because you got fooled again?

How does the "Action" step compare to what you usually do?

ACTION STEPS	WHAT I USUALLY DO
1. Use "what" and "how" questions, not "why" questions.	1. _____ _____
2. Use belly breathing.	2. _____ _____
3. Return your attention and involvement to the present.	3. _____ _____
4. Relax your body.	4. _____ _____
5. Become physically involved with your environment.	5. _____ _____
6. Make yourself more comfortable, if you can. If you can't, that's okay, it will pass.	6. _____ _____

7. Remind yourself the attack will end on its own.	7. _____ _____
8. Follow the Rule of Opposites.	8. _____ _____
9. Choose long-term freedom, not immediate comfort.	9. _____ _____
10. Make the choice that will please you four hours from now.	10. _____ _____

Step Four: Repeat

Sometimes you may start feeling better, but then feel another wave of panic. Your first reaction might be, "Oh no, it didn't work!" The "repeat" step is here to remind you that it's okay if that happens. It's not unusual or dangerous. In fact, it's a good chance to practice, which is what you need. Just take it from the top again. You may go through several cycles before the attack is over. Use each one as a chance to practice the AWARE steps.

How does "Repeat" compare with what you usually do?

REPEAT	WHAT I USUALLY DO
1. Expect and accept additional flare-ups of anxiety and panic.	1. _____ _____
2. Use these waves of panic as practice.	2. _____ _____
3. Just take it from the top and go through AWARE again.	3. _____ _____

Step Five: End

This step is here to remind you that:

- your panic attack will end
- all panic attacks end
- they end regardless of how you respond
- it's not your job to make the attack end

- Your only job is to make yourself a little more comfortable, if you can, while waiting for the attack to end, and otherwise to let yourself experience whatever feelings and thoughts come as part of the attack, while you stay in the situation and activity.

That way, the next time you panic and hear yourself thinking "Will this ever end?" you'll be ready to answer, *"Yes!"*

How does that compare to what you usually do?

END	WHAT I USUALLY DO
1. Remind yourself that it will end.	1. _____ _____
2. Make yourself a little more comfortable if you can.	2. _____ _____
3. Observe what's going on in you and around me.	3. _____ _____
4. Give it time to pass.	4. _____ _____

All the differences you've noted between AWARE and what you usually do can make up a valuable list for you. Review them periodically. Make it your goal to shift your responses more and more in the direction of the AWARE steps.

When you notice that you're responding in the "bad" old way, don't be discouraged. You've noticed it, and that's good news. That "bad" old way is what you used to do all the time without even noticing. Because you notice it now, you have the chance to make it different next time.

16

....

The Panic Diary

"You want me to *write* during a panic attack?"

I've heard that question a lot, so I know that the idea of writing during a panic attack takes a little getting used to. But it's well worth the effort. Once you get into the habit, it won't really seem as awkward or cumbersome as it does when you first consider it.

People often think they'll be too . . . well . . . panicky to write, but most people manage it pretty well. Their penmanship suffers sometimes, but that's okay. Neatness doesn't count.

Fill out the diary *during* the panic attack—you'll get much more benefit doing it that way than if you wait until later. Don't concern yourself with trying to figure out if you're panicky enough to warrant using one. Go ahead and do it. There's no penalty for completing more diaries than you need.

If you experience panic attacks while driving, it's a good idea to bring a tape recorder and speak your answers into it instead of writing them. If you have to write your answers out, obviously, pull over first.

There are two good reasons to use panic diaries—and one side effect that many people like. One reason is that it helps you observe and record important information that you might otherwise forget afterward. The diary helps you be a better detective, digging out the subtle thoughts and responses that can make the difference between a minor upset and a major attack. It's the next best thing to having a therapist accompany you, checking out how you deal with the panic and helping you figure out better ways to handle it in the future. If you rely on your memory, without writing the information down, you won't benefit nearly as much.

The second good reason is that by directing your attention to the questions it asks, the diary helps to organize your responses. When you see questions about what you're thinking, you'll be reminded of what you know about the role thoughts play in a panic attack and how you can help yourself. The overall effect of using the diary is to direct your attention to the helpful questions of "what" (is happening?) and "how" (shall I respond?).

The side benefit is that people often find the simple act of starting to fill out the diary helpful in bringing their panic level down. That's not why I recommend the diary, though. In fact, if you find that using the diary strongly interferes with the panic, at some point you might have to stop using it, so it doesn't prevent you from getting the panic practice you need. But as long as you can get adequate panic to practice with and still use the diary, consider it a bonus for the work you're doing.

Make several photocopies of the diary on the following two pages and carry one with you in any circumstances where a panic attack might occur.

Panic Diary

Date _____ Time began:_____ Time ended: _____

PANIC LEVEL: circle one

   0 1 2 3 4 5 6 7 8 9 10

SYMPTOMS:

Physical _____

_____

Thoughts _____

_____

Emotions _____

_____

Behaviors_____

_____

TYPE OF ATTACK: circle one

Anticipatory: a panic attack that occurs while you are thinking of a feared situation.

Situational: a panic attack that occurs while you are in a feared situation.

Spontaneous: a panic attack that appears to come "out of the blue." This means that you are not in a feared situation, or thinking about something fearful, when the attack occurs.

Where are you?

_____

What were you doing before the attack began?

_____

Are you alone? (If not, list who is present)

_____

_____

What were you thinking **before** the attack?

_____

_____

At the worst part of this attack, what are/were you afraid will happen **as a result** of this attack?

_____

_____

How are you talking back to the fears?

_____

_____

_____

How's your breathing? Did you remember to give one away first? Are you using belly breathing?

_____

_____

_____

What are you doing to calm yourself?

_____

_____

_____

Are you using any "self-protective" methods, such as distraction, support objects, protective rules or rituals, etc.? If so, describe. Are you willing to do without these methods?

_____

_____

_____

_____

How did the attack end?

_____

_____

_____

What was the worst thing that actually **happened to you** as a result of the attack?

_____

_____

_____

If the outcome you feared did not actually happen, to what do you attribute that?

_____

_____

Describe anything you experienced that you don't understand, never experienced before, or don't know how to handle.

_____

_____

_____

_____

How satisfied or dissatisfied are you with your response to this attack?

_____

_____

_____

Is there anything you want to do differently next time you have an attack?

_____

_____

_____

_____

_____

17

....

Anticipation

Imagine what it would be like if, periodically throughout the day at unpredictable intervals, someone stopped by to ask you questions like these:

- "What if you start sweating or blushing at the meeting?"
- "What if your heart gives out this afternoon at the mall?"
- "Wouldn't it be awful if you faint while you're making that toast for your daughter's wedding next summer?"
- "Have you thought about the conference next year out on the coast? I don't see how you can possibly get through that flight."

Actually, if you have panic attacks and phobias, something very much like that *is* happening to you. It just isn't somebody else doing it.

It's you asking questions like these of yourself.

If somebody else came by to bombard you with negative statements like these, you might get upset at first. But you'd quickly get tired of it and tell the person to bug off or avoid conversation with him. If you couldn't do that, you'd at least recognize that he was just trying to stir up trouble and take his heckling with a grain of salt.

When it's you doing the heckling, it's a little trickier.

Most people with panic and phobias think this way a lot. If you think you don't, you could be an exception, but the more likely explanation is that you're so used to this kind of self talk that you don't pay it much conscious attention.

This negative anticipation can have a powerful influence on how you feel, even when you're not consciously aware of it. The subliminal aspect of anticipation gives it power, because your body reacts to such thoughts even when you're not paying conscious attention. When your body hears you thinking about danger, it starts preparing to protect you. That response makes you feel anxious and leaves you wondering "why" you feel that way at that moment.

Unfortunately, even when you consciously notice the anticipation, you're not necessarily better off. That's because you're likely to get into an argument with your thoughts. The objective of any heckler is to disrupt your focus and get you into an argument.

You might argue for a variety of reasons. Maybe you believe the threats are realistic and worry about how to avert the catastrophes they predict. Maybe you recognize that the thoughts are exaggerated and unrealistic but still think it's important to dispute them "just to be sure." Maybe you're afraid that worry is hazardous to your health, and might even kill you, so you argue in an effort to save your life. Maybe you even think that only crazy people have odd and unrealistic thoughts, so you struggle against these thoughts as if your sanity was at stake.

Arguing doesn't make you any safer, but it does make you more anxious.

It may seem as if you're damned if you do (notice the thoughts) and damned if you don't, but it's not that bad. You just need to find a third way—some middle ground that lets you hear the thoughts and make a reasonable interpretation of what they mean without becoming embroiled in an argument with them.

Here's how you can create a third way for yourself that will take the sting out of anticipatory worry.

Understand the Nature of Anticipation

Most people don't really stop to think about the process of anticipation and what it means. They just assume it's an accurate prediction of some kind of trouble. Their unconscious attitude toward anticipatory anxiety is often something like, "If I'm this afraid now, how much worse will it be when I actually get there?"

They assume that when they arrive at the situation or activity they're anticipating, they will feel even worse and have more trouble than when they were home (or wherever) anticipating the trouble. In other words, they assume that the anticipatory anxiety is just the start. The real trouble, they think, will happen when they get there.

Based on the circumstances that characterize your panic and phobias, think of a few specific instances in which you experienced a lot of anticipatory anxiety about an upcoming event. It might be a drive across a bridge, an elevator ride, a highway trip, a party, a crowded store, or any other situation that's the focus of your anxiety. Identify two or three significant examples from your life, and then answer this question about each one.

What caused you the most trouble: the anticipation, or the actual results you experienced once you arrived at the event?

EVENTS   RESULTS

1. _____   _____

   _____   _____

2. _____   _____

   _____   _____

3. _____   _____

   _____   _____

4. _____   _____

   _____   _____

If you're like most people, you probably find that you had more discomfort from the anticipation than the actual situation. When you anticipate, you're free to imagine any kind of trouble, no matter how unrealistic. When you actually show up for the event, you're limited to reality, and reality is going to be a lot more "realistic" and easier to manage than your imagination. So your anticipation will naturally include a lot of fearful predictions that are unlikely to occur.

When you anticipate, it's easy to view yourself as the passive recipient of bad events. But when you actually show up, you have a role to play and options to choose, so you're not nearly the helpless target of fate that your anticipation describes. Getting engaged in the event in "real time" takes the anxiety level down.

If your review of your own history supports such a view—that your anticipation is usually worse than the actual outcome—then you have a powerful reminder to help you cope with the anticipation: "My anticipation is the high point of the anxiety. When I actually get there, my anxiety will go down, not up. I can look forward to that relief when I get there."

If your history shows you that your anticipation is usually worse than the actual outcome, it's proof that your anticipation is heckling, not helpful prediction. All that remains is to train yourself to treat it that way.

Step One: Get Better Radar

The first step is to improve your ability to notice your own heckling thoughts.

In days of old, before there was a national "do not call" list for telemarketers, most of us got a lot of phone calls we didn't want. We'd pick up the phone, and there would be a pause—an unusually long pause, not the kind of pause you'd get when a friend called. That was the first sign that it was a telemarketer. Their automated systems dialed so many people at once that there wasn't always a salesperson ready to talk to you right away.

Then someone would come on the line with a terrific offer like, "Do you want to save a lot of money on long distance calls?" or "Would you like to get all your magazines for free?"

By that time, you probably realized it was a sales call and treated it that way. Maybe you just hung up, maybe you listened politely while you tried to get them off the phone, or maybe you borrowed Jerry Seinfeld's idea and asked for *their* home number.

But what if you didn't realize it was a sales call instead of a giveaway? Well, you might end up buying a lot of magazines you didn't want.

It's the same thing with anticipatory worry. These thoughts contain no information you can use. If you treat a telemarketer like someone actually calling to offer you a free present, no strings attached, you're going to buy a lot of magazines and Ginzu knives. If you treat your anticipatory worries like ordinary, reasonable thoughts, you're going to buy into a lot of panic attacks. In both cases, you need to recognize the message for what it really is and respond accordingly.

Fortunately, the great majority of these anticipatory thoughts announce their arrival with the words "what if."

Step Two: See the Thought for the Symptom It Is

The typical heckling thought is filled with words of catastrophe like heart attack, stroke, faint, and humiliation. If you focus on those words, you're going to get fooled into being very upset.

But look at how the thought starts: "What if. . . ?" You know what those words mean by now, don't you?

They mean "let's pretend something bad." The thoughts don't describe something that's actually happening. They're not there to inform you. They're there to egg you on, to get you agitated. They're going to heckle you until you can't think straight.

And why are you thinking this way? Only one reason. You're nervous. These thoughts are a symptom of nervousness.

They aren't important warnings. They aren't valuable messages that can help you live a happier and healthier life. They're merely symptoms of anxiety, and they mean the same thing as all other such symptoms: "I'm nervous." Nothing more.

Don't Play the Heckler's Game

The third step is to respond in a way that soothes you, rather than letting the heckling thoughts throw you off your stride.

RESPONSE METHOD 1: LET YOURSELF BE NERVOUS

Briefly check out the thought to see if there's any new or helpful information that you haven't heard a thousand times already, something that actually suggests a way you can live a safer and healthier life. If the thought contains a reasonable way to take better care of yourself, by all means, use it.

But the overwhelming majority of heckling thoughts don't offer anything of value, just an invitation to get worried and upset. You can dismiss such thoughts by simply saying, "That's okay, I'm just nervous. It's okay to be nervous."

Sometimes, that's all it takes. Simply notice the thought, identify it as useless worry, recognize it as part of the human condition, and let it go. But other times, you will find it hard to let go of the thought. Instead of getting into a struggle with it, use one of the following response methods.

RESPONSE METHOD 2: BYPASSING THE ARGUMENT

Have you ever had the experience of dealing with a person who just likes to argue—a Democrat, if you're a Republican; a National League Fan, if you're an American League fan; somebody who just enjoys arguing for its own sake?

What could you do if you were seated next to such a person at a wedding reception and you just didn't want to argue? You want to stay for the reception, so leaving is out, and all the seats are assigned and full, so moving is out. Nobody else wants to argue with this guy, so trading seats is out as well.

What could you do? You could try changing the subject, but he might just point out that you're changing the subject and keep bringing the conversation back to arguing. You could refuse to talk, but he might confront you on that and keep trying to resume the argument. You could try and ignore him, but just the effort of ignoring him would keep him in your attention. There are a lot of things you could try, but they all involve arguing—except one: humor him. Agree with everything he says. He'll soon get bored and look for someone else to argue with.

Your anticipatory thoughts are a lot like this guy's arguing. They're repetitions of ideas that have little basis in fact. They add no value to your life, and the more you argue with them, the more persistent they become. But if you humor them, they tend to fade away.

Anticipatory thoughts are just symptoms of anxiety. It's helpful to recognize them for what they are and respond in some useful way. But you don't have to honor them, or give them more seriousness and respect than they deserve. They're the mental equivalent of trash-talking. Arguing with them will tend to get you more agitated and upset, so don't argue with them. Humor them.

Think back on some of the anticipatory thoughts listed at the beginning of this chapter.

"What if I start sweating or blushing at the meeting? (Oh, yeah, I'm gonna sweat up a storm. Better bring some mops. The sweat's gonna run through that conference room like a tidal pool at full moon. And blushing. They can turn off the lights, I'll be producing enough candlepower to light the whole room in a nice red tint!)"

"What if my heart gives out this afternoon at the mall? (Why, I'll be surprised if this old ticker takes me past breakfast!)"

"Wouldn't it be awful if I fainted while making that toast for my daughter's wedding next summer? (Faint? I'll probably fart, too, and clear out the whole restaurant. When the groom's family sees what a nut I am, they'll be calling the Pope for an annulment.)"

Humoring is a great way to steer clear of becoming embroiled with these thoughts. Simply take the thought, agree with it, and add some more exaggerated details of your own.

It's always good to try these methods first when you're not anxious. If you wait until you're anxious, it'll seem too "experimental." Try it now.

Write down two of your most frequent "what if" thoughts.

1. _____

_____

_____

2. _____

_____

_____

Now write humoring responses. Agree with the thought and add some exaggerated details of your own, just the way I did above.

1. _____

_____

_____

2. _____

_____

_____

RESPONSE METHOD 3: CALL THE QUESTION

"Call the question" is the name of a parliamentary procedure used in legislatures and other organizations to shut off debate and bring an issue to an immediate vote, so that the matter can be concluded.

Suppose you find yourself worrying about some upcoming event during which you think you might panic—perhaps driving across a bridge or meeting a friend to shop at a crowded mall—and you find that the two previous methods don't seem to help much on this occasion. The event is several days away, and you'd rather not be plagued by worry until it arrives. You realize that the anticipation is usually the worst part for you, and your history shows that once you actually tackle such an event, it's never as bad as you anticipated. But you'd like to worry less in the meantime, if that's possible.

It is. Here's how.

Immediately, or as soon as possible, go do exposure that is comparable to the task you are anticipating. For instance, if you're worrying about a bridge, go drive across the bridge. If you can't exactly duplicate what you're anticipating, such as a party or other special event, do something as comparable as possible, something that involves the same fears and the same approximate level of fear.

"Why," you might wonder, "would I ever do that?"

The reason is that the anticipation is worse than the reality. The sooner you get to the reality, the less anxiety you have to tolerate. Rather than live in dread of driving over the bridge for four days, take an extra drive on it today and get the relief that comes with completing the task that much sooner. While it may not entirely eliminate the worry you experience, it will lessen it. And, if you're willing to do more repetition, say, driving the bridge each day, you'll get all the more relief.

The three methods described above will enable you to dismiss worrisome "what if" thoughts more easily. But it will also be helpful to reduce the frequency with which you experience such thoughts. Here's a way to do that.

Reduce Your Supply of Worry

Everybody wants to worry less. But when you tell yourself, "Stop worrying," "Don't think about it!," or "Why are you worrying?" it just feeds into the worrying and makes it more persistent. Here's a method you can use to gradually reduce the amount of repetitive worry in your life.

First, let me clarify what I mean by worry. I don't mean planning, problem-solving, or any kind of thinking that produces a desired result or plan. When I say worry, I mean the unproductive and unpleasant repetition of "what if" concerns that never reach a conclusion or result in a plan. It's the kind of worry that might nag you for an hour, yet if you wrote it down on paper, it would boil down to one or two sentences, constantly repeated.

Here's what you do. Schedule two worry periods each day, ten minutes apiece. Write them in your day planner. Select two times when you can have some privacy. Avoid scheduling them first thing in the morning, last thing at night, or right after meals. During these worry periods, don't engage in any other activity like driving, showering, eating, cleaning, listening to the radio, riding on a train, etc. Instead, devote your full attention and energy to worrying and nothing else.

When it's time for a worry period, spend the full ten minutes worrying about the same things you usually worry about. You might want to make a list ahead of time, so you don't overlook any. During your worry period, indulge yourself in pure worry. Don't try to solve or minimize problems, reassure or relax yourself, or take any other positive steps with respect to the things you're worrying about. Just worry, which for most people means repeatedly reciting lots of "what if" questions about unpleasant possibilities.

Do your worrying out loud, in front of a full-length mirror.

No, that wasn't a typo. The point of worrying in this way is to help desensitize you to this worry as efficiently as possible. Most worry occurs when we're busy with something else, something that doesn't really take up our full attention. We might worry while driving, showering, doing homework, or watching a dull TV show. We never really get to give the worry our full attention. Because of this, and because we keep the worrying "in our heads," it's easy for it to continue endlessly.

When you say the worries out loud, you also hear them. And when you worry in front of a mirror, you also see yourself worrying. You're no longer just worrying in the back of your mind. Hearing and watching yourself, it's no longer subliminal. Most people find that it enables them to finish up their worrying in much less time than usual.

The main benefit comes during the rest of the day, outside your worry periods. When you find yourself worrying at other times, you will probably find it relatively easy to postpone the worries until your next worry period. You have a choice:

a) take ten minutes now to worry very deliberately about this issue, or

b) postpone it to your next worry period.

Postponing can be powerful, but only if you actually follow up and do the worry periods as prescribed. If you try to postpone worries, knowing that you won't actually do the worry period when the time arrives, you'll probably find that the postponing doesn't work for you. So don't try to fool yourself.

This technique can be an excellent addition to your exposure program. (Of course, since it's about anticipatory anxiety, don't use it during your actual exposure time.) If you'd like to try out this technique, identify a few worries that you can use in a worry period. They don't have to be realistic. The best ones to choose are the ones that bother you the most.

My Worry List

_____

_____

_____

_____

_____

_____

_____

_____

_____

_____

_____

_____

_____

My worry periods today are scheduled for _____

and_____

18
....

Creating Your Exposure Program

Are you ready to start doing exposure? Look back on what you've read and written in this workbook. Take a few minutes to reflect on the material we've covered. Then rate yourself on the following scale:

1. I've read some or all of the book but haven't done all the exercises thoroughly, and I'm undecided about making the effort.

2. I've read all the chapters carefully and done all the exercises thoroughly, but I still believe that panic is dangerous or I disagree with what I've read in some important way, and I'm unwilling to practice with panic.

3. I've read all the chapters carefully and done all the exercises thoroughly, and I'm willing to practice with panic and feel those sensations as part of the price of getting better, even though I know it will be difficult, unpleasant, and scary at times.

4. I'm not afraid. I'm ready to practice and do whatever it takes. I don't think it will be that hard.

Depending on the numerical rating you give yourself, here's what I suggest you do next.

1. Ask yourself why you haven't done a thorough job of reading the book or doing the exercises. Is it possible you're skimming through it because the subject makes you anxious? Won't you be in a better position to decide if you read the book carefully and work all the exercises thoroughly?

2. If rating #2 describes you, but you're still looking for a way to progress, consider working with a good therapist in your community who is trained in the cognitive behavioral treatment of

anxiety disorders. For suggestions about how to find such a person, visit my website at www.anxietycoach.com and check out the article called "First Steps to Recovery." Also see Resources in the back of this book for a list of internet sites that offer directories of professional therapists who specialize in treating anxiety.

3. Read on. This chapter will guide you through the process of planning a detailed recovery program.

4. Prepare yourself for the possibility that it might be more difficult than you expect. That way, you won't be tricked into thinking that you're "failing" if it proves to be harder than you thought.

To get regular practice with panic, you need a plan for Progressive Exposure. Here's how to create one:

Step One: Create a Hierarchical List of Practice Tasks

This list will be your guide to exposure. When prepared properly, it will specify all the objects, situations, and activities you need to practice with and the order in which to do them.

Start by reviewing the places, objects, and activities that you avoid, the ones you identified in Chapter 5, and select the general group you want to work on first. (I suggest that you work with one kind of activity at a time. For instance, you might choose driving, sitting in a large audience or eating in a restaurant.)

Write down as many specific instances of this activity or situation as you can. Incorporate all the factors that influence how much fear you expect to experience. Include all the relevant characteristics of the task or object you're going to work with—for instance, the type of road (for driving) or audience (for public speaking).

What about Interoceptive Exposure?

If you could arrange to practice with panic in the comfort and convenience of your own home, that would be useful too, wouldn't it? Actually, you can. One exposure technique used by some therapists is called *interoceptive exposure*. That's a ten-dollar word for deliberately creating the physical symptoms of panic—a racing heart, lightheadedness, sweating—without actually going into a phobic situation, by means of various exercises such as spinning around in a chair with wheels until you feel dizzy, running up and down stairs until you sweat and feel your heart race, inhaling through a straw to simulate labored breathing, and drinking coffee to deliberately induce anxiety. Some of these techniques are designed to tax you physically. So if you want to include them in your program, be sure to discuss them with your physician first.

For instance, with respect to driving, you should include the following variables:

- Type of road (from a major freeway to a quiet residential street)
- What lane to drive in
- Presence of construction and other delays and obstacles
- Time of day (to reflect different amounts of traffic and light)
- Distance from home
- Presence of "obstacles," such as traffic lights and left turns
- Overpasses, bridges, tunnels
- Unfamiliar roads
- Driving alone or with a passenger

With respect to sitting in an audience, your list should reflect these variables:

- Size of audience
- Composition of audience (Do you know them? Are they high-powered executives in suits, or a group of plain folks dressed casually?)
- Type of audience (movie, church, PTA meeting, all of which imply different rules of conduct. For example, how quiet are you expected to be?)
- Where you sit, with respect to distance from the door, and ease of exit
- Length of the meeting or event
- Extent of your participation, from passively watching a movie to raising your hand, asking a question, walking up to the front of the room, etc.

With respect to eating in a restaurant, you would want to address these variables:

- Size of restaurant
- Self serve versus table service
- Number of people in your party
- Who is in your party (your degree of comfort with that person or persons)
- Meal length
- Crowding factor (from waiting 20 minutes for a table to getting seated right away in an empty room)
- Fanciness factor (being served chateaubriand by Pierre may be more anxiety-provoking than burgers by Betty)
- Table location (in the center of a room, or near the back door)

Whatever activity or situation you are working on, be sure to include all the variables that can affect your anxiety level.

Rate each of these tasks on the Fear Scale of 1 to 100

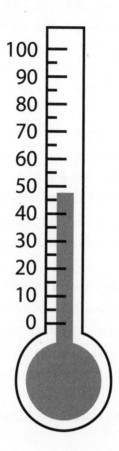

Use this scale to make your own subjective rating of how anxiety-provoking you expect each task to be. After you've rated each task in your exposure list, list them in descending order, from hardest to easiest.

Pick a starting point on your list. It could be an activity or location that you could probably tolerate but usually avoid because you don't want to impose that fear on yourself.

Now you have a hierarchy. It's undoubtedly anxiety-provoking just to write this much down, but don't let that deter you.

At various points in this process—creating your hierarchy, scheduling your exposure, doing your exposure—you will find yourself wondering "What did I do this for?" or "What did I come here for?" The answer will always be the same.

"This (the anxiety I'm feeling right now) is what I came for!" because that's what you need to practice with to get your life and your freedom back.

Here is an actual example of the beginning portion of a driving hierarchy. The person who developed it had not driven in many years, so she had to start with fundamental steps. You may not need to start with such small steps, but it's usually a good idea to include more steps, and smaller ones, than you may really need. If you check out a step and find that it produces little or no anxiety, you can move on right away, so don't be concerned with starting too small.

- Sit in car, parked in driveway, door open.
- Sit in car, parked in driveway, door closed.
- Sit in car, parked in driveway, door closed, key in ignition.
- Sit in car, parked in driveway, door closed, engine running.
- Drive car to end of driveway, and back again.
- Drive car onto street and back onto driveway.
- Drive car onto street and park there in front of house.
- Drive car several houses away, and return to driveway.
- Drive around block.
- Drive three blocks down Adams Avenue and return.
- Drive to the end of Adams Avenue and return.
- Drive three minutes east on Madison and return.
- Drive three minutes west on Madison and return.
- Drive ten minutes on Madison, whichever direction is more difficult.
- Turn right (north) onto Harlem from Madison and drive around block.
- Turn left (south) onto Harlem from Madison and drive around block.
- Drive three minutes north on Harlem and return.
- Drive three minutes south on Harlem and return.
- Drive ten minutes on Harlem, whichever direction is more difficult, and return.
- Drive fifteen minutes on Madison, one way.
- Drive fifteen minutes on Harlem, one way.

Generally I ask people to continue with such driving steps up to the point where they're driving on local roads for a round trip of an hour or so and beginning to find it a bit boring. You could then add more steps to cover various kinds of road conditions that you might fear—left turn lanes, long red lights, busier roads, roads with fewer stores and places to turn off, and so on. Be sure to include all the situations you fear. Once you reach this point, you can expand your hierarchy to include expressway driving, using the same method of small steps.

Start building your own list of steps right now:

_____

_____

_____

_____

_____

_____

_____

_____

_____

_____

_____

_____

_____

_____

_____

_____

_____

_____

_____

_____

_____

Step Two: Assess Your Use of the Self-Protective Strategies, and Make Plans to Reduce Your Reliance on Them

Most people with panic and phobias have developed a variety of ways by which they try to protect themselves from panic, including support people, support objects, protective rules and rituals, superstitions, distractions, and various ways of "fighting" the fear.

If you're really stuck and need to get started by any means necessary, these methods can help, but you pay a price for using them—one that gets more and more expensive as time goes on. Be aware that they are a temptation and can easily undo or block your progress. Minimize your use of these methods, and let go of them entirely as soon as you are able.

Step Three: Address Your Use of Medication with the Doctor Who Prescribes It

By now you should have picked up on the idea that "common sense" goes out the window in trying to overcome a phobia. Your gut reactions of what to do almost always turn toward trying to protect yourself, so they make the phobia worse instead of better. Working with exposure means overturning common sense in favor of the Rule of Opposites and finding new ways to do things.

So it is with medication. If you're using medication to treat an anxiety disorder and it's working so well that it blocks all your panic symptoms, you won't have any symptoms to which you can expose yourself. If you want to use exposure methods, you will actually need to gradually reduce your use of the medication, under the supervision of your prescribing physician, to the point where you can again feel the panic to at least a mild degree.

On the other hand, if your medication helps but doesn't prevent you from having panic attacks, you may not need to make any changes until you're further along with exposure and ready to consider slowly getting off the medication entirely.

Be sure to discuss this with your prescribing physician before making any changes and follow the guidelines he or she gives you.

Step Four: Review the Relevant Chapters in Part Four

I discuss tips and problem-solving methods for several specific phobic areas—the fears of public speaking, flying, elevators (claustrophobia), driving, and social phobia in general—in greater detail in Part Four. Be sure to read whichever of those chapters apply to you before completing a hierarchy for those problem areas.

Step Five: Schedule Your Exposure Practice Times

Here are three important guidelines for scheduling your exposure practice. Follow them to get the most benefit possible from your efforts.

1. Schedule an hour of practice five times a week, in advance, and record the specific time in your planner or calendar.

2. Stay with your schedule on "good" days and "bad," on days when you feel really confident and days when you dread it.

3. Schedule your practice as an independent activity, separate from the other components of your day. For instance, if you're working with driving, don't fold practice into shopping or other trips you have to make anyway. Exposure should be a single, separate task you do for no reason other than practice.

An hour a day seems like a lot of time, I know. That's mostly because we're talking about something you dread. If we were talking about setting aside an hour for your favorite television show or to participate in a hobby or sport, it wouldn't seem like much time at all.

Be sure to do your exposure on a schedule. Otherwise, you may be sorely tempted to do exposure only on days when you "feel like" you can handle it and to skip those days when you wake up feeling out of sorts. That would be a big mistake.

If you only do exposure on the days you feel like you can handle it, you won't leave the panic behind. You'll just reach a compromise with it, and it will continue to plague and worry you.

What if you wake up feeling anxious and sure you'll have a panic attack? Should you skip your practice that day? Of course not. Remember what the point of exposure is. It's to practice with panic, not to see if you can do exposure without panicking. When you expect you really will panic, that's all the more reason to go and practice.

One point a lot of people have trouble with is making the exposure a separate, exclusive activity. People don't like it because they're busy and want to multitask, or because it reduces their ability to distract themselves in a task. But it's very important to focus only on exposure when you're working your program. If you multitask, for instance, doing exposure in a department store while actually shopping for various items you need, you'll be motivated to "get through it" by the need to get those particular items. But "getting through it" is very different from exposure. It's not about tossing a few items in your cart and getting out of there before you panic. It's about practicing with panic.

If you're doing exposure in stores: walk through the aisles, putting items in a cart and then returning them to the shelves (or just leave the cart for the stock staff). Examine the merchandise, but don't actually do your shopping. You're not there to shop, you're there to practice with panic.

People often feel anticipatory embarrassment about walking around in a store without buying anything or repeatedly riding an elevator up and down. They expect to stick out like a sore thumb, imagining that store security will keep them under scrutiny, and worrying what to say if a store clerk offers assistance. In the rare event that anyone actually does notice you, simply respond "No thanks, I'm just browsing" or "No thanks, I'm just killing time."

If you're riding an elevator up and down, and when you reach the first floor there are people waiting to get on, they may wait for you to exit first. In that situation, just say "I'm staying on. I'm just riding!" and they get on and you resume your ride. That explanation doesn't really tell them anything, of course, about why you're riding up and down, but people don't generally cross-examine you about what you're doing. They're just offering the courtesy of letting you off first. If someone ever did ask, which hasn't happened to me in 20 years of elevator riding, I'd just say "I'm practicing with a fear of elevators," and that would be it.

Same thing with driving. Schedule practice drives that have no purpose other than exposure. Keep exposure trips separate from other trips you have to make for other purposes. If you make your visit to Aunt Dotty an exposure practice, you might be less willing to panic than you would on a pure exposure drive. Schedule your exposure so that you're as free to panic as possible.

Step Six: Progressing through Your Hierarchy

Go through your hierarchy from the starting point you select, a step at a time. As a particular step becomes boring, move on to the next step. Don't rush. If you have two consecutive days with little or no panic at a particular step, it's probably time to move up to the next step.

Review your progress once a week, and make adjustments to your schedule and hierarchy as necessary.

Evaluating Your Progress

There are a lot of tricky things about overcoming panic attacks and phobias. Here's another one. Most times, people judge how well a self-improvement project is going by how they feel. If they're getting more comfortable with a diet, an exercise plan, or a sleep schedule, they figure it's going well. And if they feel less comfortable, they take that as a sign that it's not working so well.

This method of evaluating your progress will not work with phobias. If you follow it, it will trick you into maintaining your old phobic ways. When you use exposure methods to recover from panic and phobias, you purposefully enter into anxiety-provoking situations and activities in order to desensitize yourself by becoming anxious, having panic symptoms and panic attacks, and responding in a different way than you used to. Instead of resisting the panic, avoiding it, and struggling to protect yourself, you willingly expose yourself to it, and use the AWARE steps to let it pass. In the beginning, you'll probably have more anxiety than you did when you were responding in a phobic way. So if you judge your initial progress by your comfort level, it's going to seem like you're getting worse. When you use your comfort level as a criterion by which to judge your progress with a phobia, it always tells you the same thing: "Go home—you'll feel better!" Bad advice.

You'll be much better served by using performance as the criterion by which to evaluate your success with progressive exposure in two ways:

1. "Do I show up? Do I regularly go into the activities and situations I have listed on my hierarchy?"

2. "Do I stay and follow the AWARE steps there?"

If you're performing these two key steps as I've described them, you can be confident that you are doing what it takes to make progress. Postpone any other evaluation of your success until the end of the first month of regular practice.

When Am I Done?

It's often hard to know when you're done and can cease your exposure program, declare victory, and store your diaries and notes in the attic.

You're done when you can do everything you listed in your hierarchies without panic or fearful anticipation, and when there is no longer anything you avoid for fear of a panic attack. But people frequently find it hard to "feel sure" that they're finished.

So here's a guideline. Since you can't be sure either way, engage in overkill. Do more than you need to. That will always be better than doing less than you need to. Panic disorder can be a miserable problem, and the old saying, "give it an inch and it'll take a yard" describes it well. Do more than you need to, and wait until it's really obvious that you have nothing left to overcome.

What if you're not sure whether you fear and avoid something or just don't like it? I suggest you treat it as if it's a fear, and do exposure with it. That will tell you whether your avoidance is a matter of fear or simple dislike. You'll always be better off doing more rather than less.

PART FOUR

Notes on Common Phobias

19

....

Fear of Flying

Most people who aren't afraid of flying assume that the fear of flying is all about crashing. But most people who seek help with a flying phobia aren't worried about crashing. They're afraid of having a panic attack on the airplane. They view the airplane as a kind of flying trap, one in which they will have a panic attack when they hear the door clang shut. As a result, they fear they will lose control of themselves. The end result they envision is that they will die of fright, go crazy, or act so out of control that the crew and passengers will have to subdue them and deliver them to a waiting ambulance or police car at the next airport, making a splash on the front page of their local newspaper.

Others—a smaller group, in my experience—do fear that the plane will crash. To them, flying looks inherently unsafe, untrustworthy, and experimental. These people are often familiar with detailed safety statistics showing not only that commercial flying is the safest form of transportation but also that numerous everyday activities carry far higher risks of death and injury than flying does. Yet knowing these statistics hasn't helped them overcome their fear. In fact, it adds to their frustration of experiencing this fear even though they know it is "illogical." It's often not so much death they fear, as it is the fear they imagine they would experience in the moments before death.

Most people are focused on one of these two fears, although some have a blend of both. Whether experienced separately or together, both fears are solvable problems. That's especially true because, even though these people are terribly afraid, they want to fly. This tells us something important about the fear of flying. No one seeks help with a fear of, say, jumping into the lion cage at the zoo. That would be dangerous, and the fear of doing it is your friend, helping keep you safe. People generally don't want to overcome the fears that keep them safe.

People find it hard to solve their fear of flying on their own because they have the idea that they must fight against this fear and protect themselves from it to become less afraid. But this seemingly "common sense" approach doesn't work because it plays right into the panic trick. Instead, what works with this phobia is the Rule of Opposites.

Is It Danger or Is It Discomfort?

When it comes to the fear of flying, people sometimes assume that their fear must be motivated by danger, because they're at 30,000 feet or more. People sometimes say, "You can't tell me that flying is completely safe. Crashes have happened." And that's true. Flying is not completely safe. Neither is anything else. We're living in a world in which the cumulative mortality rate is 100 percent.

Whether flying is completely safe isn't the issue. Do you regularly engage in activities that are *less* safe than flying? And do you engage in them without panic? You most certainly do. There's a long list of everyday activities more dangerous than flying. If you were simply afraid of dying, you would eliminate all other activities—such as driving, walking across busy streets, even taking prescription drugs—that carry a higher statistical danger than flying. But no one eliminates all such activities, not even the housebound agoraphobic.

The great majority of people who seek help for their fear of flying did fly many times before they became afraid. They've had enough experience with flying to determine what they fear. If you haven't flown yet, you may be struggling with "fear of the unknown," not fear of flying itself, and therefore find it hard to place yourself into one of the four groupings below. If that's the case, read the suggestions for all four groups and experiment with all the suggestions.

Let's start with the question, is your fear of flying a *signal fear* or a *conditioned fear?*

- A **signal fear** is one that accurately discriminates between safe situations and unsafe ones.
- A **conditioned fear** doesn't discriminate at all, but always sounds an alarm whether danger is present or not.

A signal fear gives me a useful warning about how I can make myself safer and discriminate between dangerous situations and relatively safe ones. A conditioned fear just tells me to be afraid but doesn't give me any useful information for living more safely.

Signal and Conditioned Fears

This illustration will help clarify the difference between signal fears and conditioned fears.

Suppose I walk through a village and pass a number of dogs—all kinds, from miniature poodles to large pit bulls and doberman pinschers. Some of them are locked inside houses, looking out of windows. Some are on leashes. Others are tied up behind securely gated fences. Some are wandering the streets on the loose.

If I have a phobia about dogs, I'll probably feel afraid of each one of them, the miniature poodle locked in the house as well as the pit bull running loose. My fear won't discriminate between the dogs that are likely to hurt me and the ones that couldn't hurt me even if they wanted to. (If I had a really severe dog phobia, I might even be afraid of toy dogs or pictures of dogs.)

That's a *conditioned fear*. It means that I've become conditioned to experience fear whenever I see a dog, regardless of whether it poses any actual danger. A conditioned fear doesn't give me any useful information about how I can be safer, nor does it give me any signal I can use to discriminate between dangerous dogs and harmless ones. A conditioned fear is like an oversensitive car alarm that rings in response to any vibration, even if it's a block away.

On the other hand, suppose I walk through the village and feel fear only when a large dog on the loose approaches me, teeth bared, fur up, and growling. When other dogs bark at me from behind a fence, or little dogs on the loose wag their tails at me, I don't feel any fear. If a stray miniature poodle growls at me, I don't feel any fear either, because I know I can easily protect myself. Only when a large, loose dog approaches me and shows signs of attack do I become afraid.

In that case, my fear discriminates among the different dogs and gives me a valuable signal that a potentially dangerous dog has approached me, and to take steps to protect myself or else I'm liable to get hurt. It also reassures me that I don't need to protect myself from other dogs. That's a *signal fear*. It's like a car alarm that only goes off if someone tries to steal my car, not whenever a heavy truck rumbles by.

Review your actual history with the fear of flying. If your fear is crashing, does your fear discriminate between planes that will crash, and planes that will arrive safely? Or do you simply get the same fear every time?

_____

_____

If your fear is losing control of yourself while on board the aircraft, does your fear make a clear distinction between panic attacks that peak and then pass and those that cause you to act (not worry that you will, but actually behave) in ways so unacceptable that you could land in jail or the hospital?

_____

_____

Based on your answer(s) above, is your fear of flying a signal fear, or a conditioned fear?

_____

_____

Which Type Are You?

People with fear of flying fall into four distinct categories based on their answers to the questions above. The differences between "types" call for different approaches to overcoming their fears.

Type 1: If you're afraid of crashing, and you believe your fear actually discriminates between the planes that will crash and those that won't, you're a "Type 1." You don't really have a reason to overcome the fear and probably don't want to. Why would anyone want to overcome a fear that accurately tells them which planes are dangerous and which aren't? That would be a useful skill, and if you had it, you would be highly sought after by the Federal Aviation Administration. If you actually believe you possess that ability, this chapter will not be of much help to you. You need to either live with the phobia and avoid flying or re-examine your belief about the signal value of your fear.

Type 2: If you're afraid of panic and have a history of actual disruptive behavior on an airplane that got you in trouble with the crew or authorities, you're a "Type 2." You should refrain from flying until you can find ways to alter the behavior that got you in trouble. Seek out a consultation with a psychologist or other mental health professional. But first review your history carefully. It's surprisingly common for people who have cried on an airplane, or shouted out when startled by turbulence, or grabbed the hand of the passenger next to them, or asked to be let off, to think that these were signs of being out of control. That's just you showing your fear, and then feeling embarrassed about it. The Type 2 category is only for people who actually got in trouble because they acted in some out-of-control way. If you just feared doing it, or showed your fear and felt embarrassed, this is not your category.

Type 3: If you're afraid of crashing and have the same fear every time you think about taking a flight, then your fear doesn't discriminate. It always says the same thing: "This plane is unsafe!" You have a conditioned fear, and that makes you a Type 3.

Type 4: If you didn't fall into any of the preceding categories, you're part of the largest group—those who have the traditional fears of a panic attack. Each time you fly, or even think about flying, you fear that you will panic on the plane and act out in some uncontrollable way. You don't actually do this when you fly, but you fear it each time regardless of your history. That's what makes you a Type 4.

Types 1 and 2 have other work to do before they're ready to desensitize themselves to flying.

If you are a Type 3 or 4, you can overcome your conditioned fears by using the methods of exposure described in Part Three and in this chapter. Yours is the traditional "fear of fear," which can be overcome by practicing with the fear.

Become More Familiar with Flying

Type 3s and some Type 4s will also need to learn more about flying. People who fear that flying is unsafe and untrustworthy often benefit from learning more about those aspects that concern them. For instance, it's common to fear turbulence, thinking it is a threat to the aircraft. I have spoken with many pilots, and without exception they've told me that turbulence is purely a matter of discomfort, not danger. They explain that the only reason they seek to move out of turbulence is because the passengers don't like it, not because it's dangerous, and that if they were flying freight, they would just ride it out. The only hazard is to passengers who ignore the "fasten seat belts" signs.

Once in a class I was presenting for fearful fliers, a guest pilot showed a photo of a jet aircraft being tested as part of the certification process. The testing included stressing various parts of the aircraft to see how much strain it would take to break that particular part. His photo showed the jet's wings bent until they pointed almost straight up at a 90-degree angle from the body of the plane. They still hadn't broken. This helped reassure class members about turbulence (especially after I explained that we wouldn't actually be flying on the plane with the bent wing!).

It's helpful to have a chat with a pilot. It reinforces the fact that there's a real live person in the cockpit, and that he or she is well trained to fly the plane and no more inclined to take risks than you are. Talking with a pilot, you'll quickly discover how well planned the entire flight process is. People often think that their questions or concerns are ones that no one has ever thought about. They figure that once they point out their safety concern to the pilot, a look of worry will cross his face, and he will immediately pull out his cellular phone to call the Federal Aviation Administration (FAA). That's just not going to happen.

For instance, what if a large bird crashed into a plane's window? Most fearful fliers think aircraft makers just put in thick glass and hope for the best. In reality, aircraft manufacturers test their designs using a gun specially designed to shoot turkey carcasses at the plane's windows and engines to make sure they can withstand bird collisions.

Another example involves fuel and refueling. People will sometimes say they heard about a flight that had to refuel because it was "running low on fuel." This naturally makes them anxious, thinking that a plane might actually run out of fuel. But as any pilot can tell you, commercial flights are required to maintain sufficient fuel so that, if their destination airport is unavailable for landing due to weather, they can fly to their first alternate airport, get turned away because of weather there too, and then fly on to their second alternate airport, land, and still have a reserve of fuel. That's how many duplicative safeguards are built into the system.

Another common question people ask pilots is, what are the chances of a mechanic having a "bad day" and maybe skipping or mishandling some key element of maintenance. They're relieved to hear that the rules require different mechanics to work on each engine, and that additional supervisory inspections and signoffs are also required, providing multiple backups for every safety procedure.

Finding a Friendly Pilot

In short, Type 3s and some Type 4s should make the effort to talk with a pilot as part of their recovery work. Try to find a commercial pilot who is willing to talk with you and maybe answer a few questions you have. If there is a class for fearful fliers in your area, it will probably include such a meeting with a pilot. If not, here are some other ideas to try:

- Call some airlines that fly out of a nearby airport, and ask if they offer programs for fearful fliers or opportunities to meet a pilot in a public information setting.
- Call airports in your area and ask if they offer any airport tours for the general public. Such tours often include a presentation by a pilot.

- If you work for a firm that has an Employee Assistance Program, contact them and ask if the EAP of a local airline can connect you with a pilot who's willing to chat with you.

- Is there an aerospace museum in your area? It might have a pilot there to answer questions. For instance, in the Museum of Science and Industry in Chicago, there's an airplane exhibit staffed by retired pilots who are there for the express purpose of answering questions.

- Check with friends and relatives to see if anyone knows a pilot who might be willing to chat.

When you do get a chance to talk with a pilot, make the most of it. Don't hedge. Don't hold back and try to get answers without revealing your fear of flying. Tell the pilot that you're afraid of flying and that's why you want to hear about flying from the pilot's perspective.

You may also want to read an entire book on the subject. See Resources at the end of this book.

Exposure and Desensitization

Whether you're a Type 3 or a Type 4, as long as yours is a conditioned fear, the main task remaining is to decondition yourself. This means, literally, practicing with the fear.

In classes for fearful fliers, I follow a simple model. Four meetings are devoted to helping people learn and practice ways of working with their fears of what might happen on the airplane as well as their anticipatory fears on the ground. Then we go on a flight together so that people can practice what they've learned. They deliberately expose themselves to the fears they anticipate, and the exposure lessens the fears.

A businessman in one such class told me, "Dr. Carbonell, I flew more than 100,000 miles last year. That's probably more than you did. I was more afraid the last mile than I was the first. How is more flying going to help?"

He had a good point. More flying of the same kind doesn't help. He needed exposure to flying in circumstances where he could practice different ways of responding to his anxiety. Continued repetition of the same old "white knuckle" flying would be of no help to him.

A Different Kind of Flying

People who are afraid of flying have usually developed a variety of ways to try to be unafraid. They resist the passive role of passenger and try to control things.

Type 3 people, who fear crashing, try hard to feel as if they were at least monitoring key aspects of the flight and perhaps making themselves safer. They may also get their business affairs in order and review their will, insurance policies, and so on before a flight. They may go to church and light a candle or say a prayer. They may seek additional information about their aircraft, such as its age and manufacturer, and try to pick a "winner." They may try to select a flight based on superstitious ideas about lucky flight numbers, dates, and the like.

Even their worrying is an effort to control things, as if they could somehow influence the outcome by thinking about it enough. People often have superstitious ideas about worrying that lead them to worry more. For instance, people sometimes believe—or half-believe—that something bad is more likely to happen to them if they don't worry about it ahead of time. This leads them to worry about bad events as a form of insurance. If they worry, they figure, that makes it less likely to happen.

None of these thoughts or actions influence the aircraft. All of them tend to make people more nervous, not less. So Type 3 flyers tense up their bodies, breathe shallowly, and do all the things that increase their anxiety level instead of decreasing it.

Type 4 flyers, who fear in-flight panic attacks and the consequences they imagine will follow, also strive for control, but their efforts are aimed at themselves. They want to control their fears. They struggle to feel unafraid. They try desperately to hide their fear from others and to distract themselves from their fear—making the anxiety worse, not better.

A practice flight is a good way to let yourself work with the experience of being afraid. Refrain from your usual control strategies, interrupt yourself when you notice you're using them, and use the flight as a chance to feel the anxiety and accept it.

Even though you've read about how progressive exposure works, when it comes down to actually boarding the plane for your practice flight, you may still find yourself asking, "Why would I purposefully allow myself to be afraid and to panic?" The answer, of course, is: *Because the more you fight, resist, and hide your fear, the more persistently phobic you become. The more you allow yourself to become afraid, and to work with your fears in an accepting manner, the more readily you will lose your fear of feeling afraid. Once that happens, and you're no longer afraid of having a panic attack, the panic attacks themselves tend to fade away.* And if that nagging little voice persists, asking "What makes it safe or okay to let myself be afraid, and to panic?" keep in mind that the answer is: *The fact that nothing dangerous happens to you when you panic.*

Working with the Claustrophobic Fears

Type 4 people, whose fear is principally of having a panic attack on the plane, are up against the classic "fear of fear" that we've discussed throughout this book.

If, besides flying, you have panic attacks in other circumstances that you have not yet resolved, I suggest you start by working with one of the other, non-flying situations first. The reason is simply that, while the claustrophobic fears of flying are treatable by the general methods of exposure, there are fewer ways to break it into small steps than there are with other phobic situations such as driving or shopping. Flying on a commercial jet simply requires more planning, time, and expense than most other activities.

This doesn't have to prevent you from making progress with flying. The work you do with other panic-inducing situations will help you when you move on to flying. Of course, if flying is the only situation in which you have panic attacks, start with that.

When you use exposure methods for any particular phobia, there are always special circumstances that you need to take into account. Let's consider how you can do that for the fear of having a panic attack aboard a commercial airplane.

Start by remembering that exposure, desensitization, and all the cognitive behavioral methods for reducing fear are based on the central idea of *reducing fear by practicing with it*. People tend to approach the fear of flying with the idea that first, while they're still on the ground, they will learn how to fly without being afraid. Then, they hope, they will fly in comfort and serenity.

But that's not how it works. In fact, that idea makes recovery far more difficult, if not impossible. The way it does work is this. You learn some methods for responding to the fear that will help calm you down rather than get you into a fight with the anxiety. Then you take a short flight somewhere, let yourself get afraid, and practice using the methods you've learned. You need practice with fear, rather than protection from it.

Your Practice Flight

The practice flight in my fearful flyer class is not a special flight—we buy seats on a regularly scheduled commercial jet for a round-trip flight to a city about an hour away. Participants just go in and sit "with the normal people," as my clients usually put it. Working on your own, you'll need to arrange your own practice flight. Even if you've been flying a lot and racking up frequent flyer miles, you're going to need to practice flying with a different set of rules than the ones you've been using. There are two important things to keep in mind about a practice flight.

1. **This is not a test.**

> The purpose of the flight is to get some practice. Participants in fearful flyer classes often start with the idea that it's a "test"—that since we're approaching the end of the class, it's time for the final exam, to see if they can fly without becoming afraid.

> That's not the idea. In fact, that's the opposite of the idea. It's practice, not a test.

> Let's pause for a moment and play a word association game, okay? What comes to mind when I offer you the word…

"TEST"

Your thoughts:

_____

_____

_____

_____

> Do you think about being graded on your performance? About passing or failing? Most people do. But the purpose of your practice flight isn't to give some students high marks and flunk others. There is no such thing as passing or failing grades in this kind of work. When kids have a fire drill at school, they don't pass or fail. They practice a routine so it will come more naturally. In the same way, your practice flight is a chance to practice.

2. **You're practicing with fear.**

> It's important to keep in mind what you are practicing when you take this flight. It's not "flying practice." Leave the flying to professionals—the pilot, flight crew, ground crew, air traffic controllers and lots of other personnel. You're just along for the ride.

> Your practice flight is about practicing with fear—getting afraid and responding in the new ways you're learning with the help of this book. You're not supposed to be fearless on your practice flight. You're supposed to work with your fear in new ways so that it subsides over time, permitting you to fly more calmly.

ARRANGING YOUR PRACTICE FLIGHT

When you feel ready to take a practice flight, schedule one specifically for that purpose. Don't just practice on a regularly scheduled business trip or a family vacation. You'll have other responsibilities on those trips, and they will leave you feeling that it might not be a good idea to "take the chance" of letting yourself get afraid or trying these newfangled ideas. It's better to specifically schedule a trip for which you have no other reason to go than to practice with your fear of flying.

Here's how to select your first practice flight:

Start by making a list of all the aspects of flying that influence how afraid you become. Here's a sample list of factors that often influence the amount of fear a person expects. **Put a check mark beside the ones that apply to you, and add your own.**

❏ length of the flight

❏ size of the plane

❏ how crowded the plane is likely to be (peak or non-peak flight times)

❏ flying over water or not

❏ daytime versus nighttime flight

❏ airline

❏ seat location (window, aisle, or middle; front or back)

❏ alone or with a support person

_____

_____

_____

_____

_____

_____

For your first flight, pick a flight that minimizes most or all of those factors so that you're starting off with as small a step as you can.

As you read this, you may experience a reaction to the mere idea of scheduling a flight. Most people do. Even before they've made a decision about whether or not to book a practice flight, most people become anxious at the very thought of it, because they, like all of us humans, have the capacity to anticipate trouble. And when we do, we experience the same emotions and physical sensations that we would experience if we were actually having trouble instead of just anticipating it.

Big Plane or Small Plane?

In these pages, I refer to taking your practice flight on a "commercial jet." But sometimes people begin their flying exposure by riding in a small private plane. Although that's fine for starters, it's important to compare the details of your fears with the characteristics of a small private plane. For a lot of people, the biggest obstacle they face is their fear about being unable to get off the airplane if they feel panicky. If that's your fear, riding in a small plane piloted by a friend won't be the kind of practice you need, because you could always ask him or her to take you back down. On the other hand, if you're one of those people whose fear is of flying itself—being high above the ground—a ride in a small plane will exaggerate the experience, which could be scarier than is necessary to work with your fears. Of course, if the phobia you're trying to overcome is limited to riding in small aircraft, this is the place to start.

For most people who have a fear of flying, this anticipatory anxiety is the most difficult part. It keeps them from getting on the plane in the first place. Yet if they could just get on the plane and have the opportunity to work with the anxiety, they *would* make progress, because once they step aboard the plan, all that's left to deal with is reality. Compared to the emotional and physical reactions brought on by all the fantastic, unrealistic, impossible scenarios your anticipation can concoct, coping with reality is a snap.

Anticipation is like a "scary movie theater" in your mind. Don't let it bluff you into retreat. Expect to have a lot of anticipatory anxiety as you prepare for your practice flight. Keep in mind that such anxiety is simply you being nervous, not a travel advisory from God. Letting yourself be afraid, and practicing with fear, may be new ideas, and though you've accepted them logically while reading this book, accepting them viscerally may take a little more experience. As your basic guide for dealing with anticipatory anxiety, use the suggestions in Chapter 17.

PREPARATIONS FOR THE PRACTICE FLIGHT

The main goal of your practice flight is to work with, rather than against, your fears. So I don't want you to distract yourself from your fears, as this feeds into the idea that you're only okay as long as you don't think about them. That limits your recovery.

1. **Make a list of the symptoms you expect to experience on board the aircraft.** Divide it by the four kinds of symptoms we discussed in Chapter 6—thoughts, emotions, physical sensations, and behaviors. I suggest you work on this over several days, as

you will probably not remember everything the first time you put pen to paper. Once you have your list of symptoms, put them on the Symptom Inventory form on page 197. List your symptoms down the left side of the page, arranged by type. Make two copies—one for the outbound flight, one for the return. You can use these to keep track of how often you experience each symptom on board the plane. Each time you notice, say, shallow breathing, you can check another box on the page. Keeping a count of your symptoms helps you cultivate an accepting attitude toward the symptoms instead of just hoping you don't experience them. As you notice the specific symptoms, you can then decide how you want to respond to them. You'll be much less likely to get caught up in a struggle to distract yourself or to prevent the symptoms.

2. **Get some graph paper and bring a sheet on each flight. On the left side of the graph paper, write in the range of values on the Fear Scale** (page 171) from 0 to 100 by tens. The bottom scale is time. Start scoring your anxiety level 10 or 20 minutes before you board the plane and continue to score it throughout the flight. Do the same on the return trip. Again, the point of this exercise is to help you cultivate an accepting, observing attitude toward your fear, because it's okay to be afraid—that's why you're on the plane.

3. **Also bring along a 5x7 card and write on it a few key phrases and ideas that you found particularly useful in this book** (or any other source you're using)—for instance, "Is it discomfort or is it danger?" or "Breathe!" This card will serve as a reminder of a few key ideas that may prove useful in those moments when you might be so afraid that your concentration and memory aren't working as well as you'd like. You won't have to remember—the ideas will be on that card waiting for you.

4. **Pack other items that will be helpful for you.** Bring several copies of the **Panic Diary** form, along with photocopies of the **AWARE steps** and the **self-hypnosis steps**. If you think you're liable to cry, bring tissues. I don't encourage people to bring "distraction tools," such as a checkbook to balance or a novel to read. The more distraction you employ, the less exposure and desensitization you're getting. But do what you have to do. If you're not willing to make your first flight without a particular object, bring it along and use it as sparingly as you can. Maybe you'll be able to leave it home the next time. People who use

anti-anxiety medications such as Xanax, Valium, or Klonopin often ask if they should bring their pills. In the beginning flights, I suggest bringing them and having them available as a backup if needed, but refraining from taking them just before the flight. If you feel protected by your meds, it will reduce the amount of fear practice you get. As you progress, you can look forward to flying without them. Avoid alcoholic beverages on the flight or just before it; they too defeat the purpose of the exposure.

5. **If you like, ask your family or loved ones to prepare a surprise for you**, some kind of small package you can open during the flight. Drawings by your kids, a gag gift or funny card, or some message of encouragement would be good.

6. **Don't forget to pack your ticket.** And bring this book as well. If you haven't flown for a while, contact the airline to make sure you're aware of the items you need for boarding, the security procedures, the time you should arrive at the airport, and so on.

THE WEEK (AND NIGHT) BEFORE

You're going to be afraid, especially if this is your first flight in a while. That's okay. When you find yourself asking "What am I doing this for?" have the answer ready. You're doing this so you can practice with the fear and get over your phobia.

Follow the suggestions for anticipatory anxiety in Chapter 17, especially the use of worry periods during the week or two prior to the flight.

I've previously mentioned some of the things people do in an effort to control their anxiety before a flight, such as monitoring the Weather Channel, preparing their wills, and so on. Make as thorough a list as you can of the ways in which you try to take control of the situation. Then let them go. Confine yourself to the role of a passenger. **What do you do?**

_____

_____

_____

_____

_____

_____

_____

You're likely to sleep poorly the night before the flight. That's not unusual, and it's not a problem. It's important for the pilot to get a good night sleep, but if a passenger doesn't, that's okay. Plan on being afraid the night before, the morning of your flight, and on your way to the airport. There's nothing you need to do about it, it's entirely predictable that you'll feel this way, so just let it happen.

Have a plan for getting to the airport. Will you go by yourself or with company? Will you drive your car, have a friend or family member drive you, or take a cab, bus, or airport shuttle? Select a plan that makes it easiest for you to get on the plane without creating obstacles for yourself. You can always change your mind and decide not to go, but don't build alibis or excuses into your planning.

Waiting at the gate will be another source of anxiety. To minimize this, board as soon as the flight is ready. Some people prefer to wait until the very last moment, to spend less time on a stationary plane but this actually adds to their nervousness. Don't wait at the gate, continuing to review your decision to fly and wondering whether you should just leave the airport. You have no new information on which to base a decision, so this kind of thinking is really just worrying, not problem-solving. The best way to respond to that worrying is to board the airplane—and thereby "call the question."

That won't entirely end your internal debate. You'll probably entertain thoughts about disembarking until the door closes and the plane pulls away from the gate. But it usually helps to move the process forward and get on the plane, where you have a reality to deal with instead of just your own anticipatory thoughts.

WAITING FOR TAKEOFF

As you get on board and pass the flight attendant, say hello and mention that you're afraid of flying. The point of this is not to ask the crew to do anything in particular—there isn't much they can do—but to break the habit of trying to keep it a secret, which makes you more self-conscious and thus more anxious. It's okay to be afraid of flying, no need to hide it.

Very often the attendant will try to be helpful, maybe coming back later to see how you're doing and perhaps offering a bit of advice or reassurance. It may be helpful—or maybe not, especially if they try to help you feel less anxious, when you're actually there to practice with your anxiety. Follow their advice only if it makes sense to you.

On one class practice flight, for instance, crew members suggested to my fearful flyer group that they distract themselves. "Keep talking to each other, and close the blinds!" one flight attendant urged. Realizing that this advice was the opposite of what we were there to do, we thanked her for the support—and followed our own plans.

For most people, the few minutes (that seem like hours) while waiting to take off are the hardest. As long as the plane remains on the ground, your anxious review of your options (Should I get off? What if I can't take it?) may continue and even intensify. If this is the hardest time for you, awareness of that fact can be helpful. Knowing that you're in the worst moments of the experience, you can sit back, breathe, remind yourself that soon you'll feel at least a little better, and be a passenger who waits.

During the Flight

What makes your practice flight extraordinary is that mission—to allow yourself to be anxious. This goes against all your instincts and habits, so you will repeatedly find yourself trying to resist the anxiety or distract yourself from it. Again and again, you'll find yourself gripping the armrest, holding your breath or breathing shallowly, arguing with yourself, watching for signs of trouble, watching the faces of the crew, trying to distract yourself, and so on. Don't let it exasperate you. The fact that you catch yourself in the act of protecting against the anxiety, or distracting from it, is good news. You've probably been doing that kind of thing for years. What's new is that now you're noticing it, and that's good. Until you notice a habit, you don't stand much chance of changing it. Congratulate yourself each time you catch yourself in the act of self-protection or distraction. Then get back to the business at hand—allowing yourself to be anxious.

Throughout the flight, keep your anxiety level graph and count your symptoms. Periodically go through the AWARE steps as you feel the need. Whenever you feel so panicky that you wonder if you should fill out a diary form, do it.

Remember, you experience fear as four different types of symptoms: physical sensations, thoughts, emotions, and behaviors, so divide your coping responses into the same categories. As in all phobic situations, keep in mind the Rule of Opposites: Every time you catch yourself in the act of resisting, switch to an accepting response.

For physical sensations, your principal coping responses will include: belly breathing, relaxation with self-hypnosis, stretching, tensing, and relaxing affected muscles, and getting up and moving around the aircraft when the pilot says you can do so.

Using the panic diary and symptom inventory will sometimes bring a sensation to your conscious attention so that you can then deal with it directly. When you experience unpleasant or scary thoughts, your first instinct will be to quarrel with them, refute them, or distract your mind from them. When you notice yourself resisting, make a note on your symptom inventory of both the resistance and the thought you're resisting. Then go back to your AWARE steps.

Develop an awareness for the "what if" thoughts that may be inviting you to "pretend something bad." Those thoughts are okay as long as you realize you're pretending.

Don't struggle in silence and isolation. Talk to your companion if you have one, or to the crew and other passengers. Above all, whenever you get anxious, remind yourself that this is what you're here for, and practice your use of the AWARE steps.

People often want to use thought-stopping techniques. One classic technique is when you find yourself worrying, you snap a rubber band on your wrist and say (to yourself) *"STOP."* The trouble is, techniques like this involve too much resistance. If you want to use it, limit yourself to one or two snaps. If it's going to work at all, it'll work with one or two snaps. Don't raise welts on your arms.

For phobic behaviors such as grabbing the seat, holding your breath, avoiding the view out the window, monitoring the engines, and so on, one simple response rule applies: do the opposite. Let go of the armrest and allow yourself to sit unrestricted; do belly breathing; look out the window; get involved in a conversation instead of listening to the engines.

When it comes to negative emotions such as fear and embarrassment, allow yourself to feel whatever you feel. Note it in your journals and other observational tools. Remember that these feelings are what you came for, and that the only way around them is right through them. Don't resist them—just give them time to subside.

Once you've had your first practice flight and are satisfied you're moving in the right direction, I suggest you fly like this at least once every three months for the first year to build a good recovery. Once will not be enough. If you fly once and wait a year or more for the next flight, you may find that the fear has regrouped. Stay with it.

Symptom Inventory

PHYSICAL SENSATIONS

_____ □□□□□□□□□□□□□□□□□□□□□□□□

_____ □□□□□□□□□□□□□□□□□□□□□□□□

_____ □□□□□□□□□□□□□□□□□□□□□□□□

_____ □□□□□□□□□□□□□□□□□□□□□□□□

_____ □□□□□□□□□□□□□□□□□□□□□□□□

_____ □□□□□□□□□□□□□□□□□□□□□□□□

_____ □□□□□□□□□□□□□□□□□□□□□□□□

THOUGHTS

_____ □□□□□□□□□□□□□□□□□□□□□□□□

_____ □□□□□□□□□□□□□□□□□□□□□□□□

_____ □□□□□□□□□□□□□□□□□□□□□□□□

_____ □□□□□□□□□□□□□□□□□□□□□□□□

_____ □□□□□□□□□□□□□□□□□□□□□□□□

EMOTIONS.

_____ □□□□□□□□□□□□□□□□□□□□□□□□

_____ □□□□□□□□□□□□□□□□□□□□□□□□

_____ □□□□□□□□□□□□□□□□□□□□□□□□

BEHAVIORS

_____ □□□□□□□□□□□□□□□□□□□□□□□□

_____ □□□□□□□□□□□□□□□□□□□□□□□□

_____ □□□□□□□□□□□□□□□□□□□□□□□□

_____ □□□□□□□□□□□□□□□□□□□□□□□□

_____ □□□□□□□□□□□□□□□□□□□□□□□□

_____ □□□□□□□□□□□□□□□□□□□□□□□□

_____ □□□□□□□□□□□□□□□□□□□□□□□□

20

....

Public Speaking

The fear of public speaking is probably the most common fear of all, more common even than the fear of death. As David Letterman has pointed out, this means that the average person going to a wake would rather be the deceased than the person giving the eulogy! But this fear is just as treatable as any other.

In this chapter, I suggest some ways you can fine-tune the methods described in this book specifically to help you overcome the fear of public speaking. The problem has three components that you will need to target: anticipation, avoidance, and self protection.

The Anticipation Trick

Here's a good question with which to start your work on fear of public speaking:

What happens to your anxiety level once you start speaking to a group, after you've been speaking for a minute or two? Does your anxiety level . . .
- ❑ Increase?
- ❑ Decrease?
- ❑ Stay the same?

If you're like most people with this fear, your anxiety level goes down, if only slightly, once you start speaking. That doesn't mean it goes away, nor does it mean it's not a problem. But it's important to notice this phenomenon. Most people respond to their anticipatory anxiety as if it were a warning of worse times ahead. They respond as if it means that they will feel worse and even more anxious once they start talking. "If I'm this afraid now," they think, "how much worse will it be once I get up there in front of everybody?"

Even people who have given many presentations despite this fear and have a clear history of their anxiety diminishing once they start talking still tend to respond as if their anticipation were a warning of more trouble ahead. They assume that the more anxious they are just before the presentation, the worse they're going to do.

That's usually not true. It assumes that your anxiety in the last few hours before you're introduced is an accurate prediction of trouble ahead and that your anxiety level will keep going up throughout the speech. *The opposite is usually true.* The high point of public speaking anxiety is often just before the speech, and the anxiety level usually decreases from that point on.

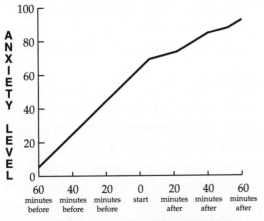

Graph 1: DAY OF PRESENTATION

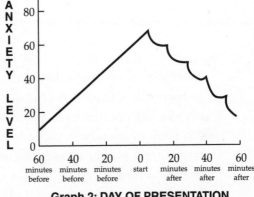

Graph 2: DAY OF PRESENTATION

Graph 1 shows the pattern most people with this phobia assume to be true in the moments before a presentation. They fear and dread the start of it, expecting that their anxiety will worsen until they're unable to continue. But for the great majority of them, Graph 2 more accurately reflects their actual experience. Their anxiety goes down, at least a little, once they get started. If you discover that this is true for you, it reveals an important way the panic trick keeps you afraid of public speaking. It leads you to believe that things will get worse, even though they will actually get better. No wonder you want to avoid it.

If Graph 2 describes the actual pattern of your fear, then our anticipatory anxiety is *not* a warning that the worst is about to come. To the contrary, your anticipatory anxiety *is* the worst part. The challenge you face, therefore, will be to accept and wait out the anticipatory anxiety, knowing that it's a sign of better moments ahead.

It will help to remind yourself to *look forward to the start of your talk*, when the anticipatory phase will be over and your anxiety level will start going down as you become actively engaged in your role. Although at first it may go down just a little, with the help of the methods in this chapter, it will likely go down much more.

I understand that it's certainly a lot easier for me to say this than for you to do it. But have modest expectations and focus on reminding yourself of this, not on how you feel at the moment or even how much you think you can believe it. Simply remind yourself that the anticipation is the worst of it, and resign yourself to letting it pass so that you can get to the next phase. Looking forward to the start of your talk can be the first of many steps to help you solve your fear of public speaking.

Of course, anticipation doesn't only start the morning of your presentation. For public speaking, it may start the moment someone asks you to give a talk, even if it's months away. Anticipation will fill the time available. To work with the more general problem of anticipation in the days, weeks, and months ahead of a presentation, you can apply the methods described in Chapter 17.

Avoidance

If the fear of public speaking causes trouble in your life, avoiding presentations and speeches will only make it worse. It's true that avoidance works okay for people who are rarely, if ever, called upon to speak in public. But if you're reading this book to learn how to get over the fear of speaking to groups, chances are you've tried avoidance and you're not satisfied with the results. Maybe it rubs you the wrong way to be afraid of public speaking, and overcoming this fear would give you personal satisfaction or help your career. Or maybe the problem is that you've become successful in your career and now that you're getting a lot of demands for your knowledge, you find it hard to resist the requests for you to share it with groups of interested people.

As with other phobias, the secret to overcoming the fear of public speaking is practice. To start practicing, locate a Toastmasters chapter in your community.

Naturally, you'll feel nervous about going to Toastmasters for the first time, the same way people working to overcome their fear of flying feel nervous about the first practice flight. Remember that you solve the fear of public speaking not by finding some way to "get rid" of the anxiety before you give any speeches—that's how you remain phobic, not how you overcome it—but by finding ways to work with the fear. So when you feel anxious about taking this step, remember that the anxiety is not a threat or warning. Rather, it's a reminder that you're on the right track.

You can generally just drop by a Toastmasters meeting as an observer, but call the club president before you visit for the first time. Use the call to introduce yourself, to check their schedule, and to learn a little about the club and what to expect. If you want to observe without participating in any way, ask whether you can.

Join a Public Speaking Club

Toastmasters is a national, nonprofit club for people who want to get better at public speaking. It's easy and inexpensive to join. You will find their contact information under Resources in the back of this book, and you can use it to find clubs in your area. It's not exclusively or specifically for people who fear public speaking, but many members join for that reason. People who don't fear public speaking join too, to improve their presentation skills, to network, and to have fun.

Toastmasters will not teach you how to overcome the fear of public speaking. But Toastmasters is a great place to practice and develop your speaking skills in front of people who play no other role in your life. People are often reluctant to try new methods in work situations and prefer to make their first attempts in situations that "don't count" as much as work does. Toastmasters offers you the opportunity to practice in a context that won't affect your job or your standing in the community.

Toastmaster clubs vary considerably. If there is more than one in your area, visit several. Some are oriented toward professional and business speakers who want to become really excellent at speaking, and others have a much more casual atmosphere. Look around to find one that feels comfortable for you.

Some goals of Toastmasters may not be relevant to you. For example, Toastmasters encourages members to reduce the use of "ahh" and "umm" in their speeches. This is more important for people who want to become really good speakers and less important for people who just want to overcome the fear of speaking. Keep your own personal goals in mind and, when they vary from the Toastmasters goals, go with yours. You'll find Toastmasters to be an encouraging and welcoming organization.

Toastmasters is a great place to practice progressive exposure because they have a range of speaking activities, from very brief tasks such as telling a joke to speeches of twenty minutes or more, and many steps in between. At some point, once you have joined a club and attended a while, you can make a speech there in which you introduce yourself to the group. This is a great opportunity to explain why you're there, to describe the fear you have, and at the same time to practice exposure and self-disclosure, rather than avoidance and hiding.

The Role of the Speaker

The next step toward solving the fear of public speaking is to clarify what your role is. Most people with this fear think of public speaking as a performance and think that the audience is there to evaluate and judge their performance. If this is how you see it, let me suggest an alternative way to think about it: most public speaking is just talking, not performing.

When the President of the United States gives a State of the Union Address, that's a performance. When a motivational speaker fills Madison Square Garden and comes out to give the keynote speech, that's a performance. But for most of us, in most situations where we're called upon to give a presentation, it's an occasion for us to talk, not perform. We're not there because we're professional speakers who make a living that way, but because we have some information that someone else wants to hear.

When you're afraid of public speaking, it's easy to think that people are watching to see how you handle the crowd and the occasion, to make personal judgments about you, and above all to see if you look nervous. But that's not usually why the audience turns out.

The better you understand your role and occupy just that role, the easier it will be to accept and let go of the anxiety. *Public speaking is just talking. Your role is speaker, not performer.* A performer might have to be eloquent and polished, but a speaker can just get up there and give people information on the announced topic.

When people assume that they have to give a performance, they make some other assumptions as well. Check these out, and see if you share any of them:

Speaking of Fear

The first time I gave a presentation at a national conference of the Phobia Society of America, I was excited but preoccupied with how I would do. Without realizing it, I thought of it as a performance. I looked out at a pretty good-sized crowd, saw people in the audience I recognized as well known experts in the field, and immediately went into "performance mode."

By that I mean that I defined the situation as one in which all those people in the audience were there to see, hear, and judge *me*. It was going to be "Dave Carbonell Day." Compared to all the presentations I've given before and since, this was by far my least enjoyable public speaking experience.

Nothing terrible happened. The audience seemed to like it well enough. Nobody booed. But throughout, I was more concerned with what the audience might be thinking about me than I was with what I had to say to the audience.

That's an uncomfortable way to give a presentation. I felt disappointed for several days thereafter and kept thinking of all the ways it could have been better. I dismissed the praise I received as charity, rather than honest feedback.

The fact is they weren't there to see me. They were just there to hear the talk about "The Therapeutic Use of Humor in the Treatment of Panic Disorder and Agoraphobia," and I happened to be the one giving it. Most of them—perhaps except my mom—would have come had the speaker been somebody else.

They were there for the material, not me.

- The audience is there principally to form an opinion of me, the speaker.
- The opinion the audience forms of me will have an important impact on me, my future, and my well-being.
- The audience is likely to form a negative opinion of me.

Sometimes these are accurate. If you're a representative from a big company's Human Relations Department speaking to employees who are being downsized, you probably *do* face an angry audience that's ready to dislike you. If you're a professor presenting your research to the faculty at a university where you're seeking employment, they probably *are* there to form an opinion of you, and it could be vital to your future. But in the majority of public speaking occasions, these assumptions are exaggerated and untrue.

Some businesspeople I work with feel strongly that they are being judged whenever they present, that virtually everything they do is factored into perceptions of their ability and future career path, and that their competitive peers are always looking for a weakness to exploit. This can be true. But even when it is, that doesn't mean you will be better off by struggling to be unaffected by such circumstances. If you face a hostile audience, you will be better served by accepting that this is the case, recognizing that it's reasonable to feel nervous about it, and allowing yourself to feel nervous without interpreting that as a bad sign. You may well be better off by coming across as open and disarming, rather than striving for a perfect defense.

The truth is, nervous speakers tend to overestimate the degree to which the audience is waiting to pounce. In most instances, speakers assume they are being judged, not because the assumptions are true, but because they are nervous. The person most likely to be forming negative opinions of the speaker is . . . guess who? The speaker.

If this is true for you, it's very helpful to know it so that you can make adjustments in your attitude toward your self-criticism and resulting anxiety. Pick a talk or presentation you gave during which you had significant anxiety, and answer the following questions about that event.

Feedback you received from others about the talk:

_____

_____

_____

_____

_____

Your own impressions of that talk:

_____

_____

_____

_____

_____

Did your impressions differ from the feedback you received? If so, how do you explain that difference?

_____

_____

_____

_____

It's common to be your own worst critic. If you see that you consistently give yourself worse reviews than you get from others, don't assume that means you're being more accurate. Consider the possibility that you're being more critical because you felt self-conscious. Also consider what kind of feedback you usually give other speakers. How does it compare to your own self-evaluations? Do you see a tendency to be more negative toward yourself than toward others?

Challenge versus Threat: Interpreting the Anxiety

So there you are in front of a group, and you're feeling nervous. Your nervousness manifests itself in a variety of ways. You feel physical sensations such as warmth, weakness, a racing heart, and so on. You engage in nervous behaviors such as shallow breathing. You feel the emotion of fear. And, most importantly, your mind is continually trying to make sense of all this and tell you what's happening.

Your mind's conclusion is likely to be wrong.

Your mind is going to notice how anxious you are, then notice the people in front of you and decide you're afraid because you're threatened somehow. If you think of this situation as a threat, and try to treat it as such, you will get enmeshed in the old panic trick. You'll feel discomfort but respond as if it were danger. Your body will prepare you for fight, flight, and freeze options. And you'll feel worse.

Do you know why it's such a stereotypical tradition to start a speech with a joke? And why that joke is usually referred to as an icebreaker?

It's because almost everybody feels anxious when they start talking to a group. Humor is a way to defuse some of that discomfort. The icebreaker gets you past treating the anxiety as a threat.

Just as treating anxiety as a threat makes it worse, treating it as a challenge makes it better.

Responding to the Challenge

The people who develop a phobia for public speaking are the ones who get into the habit of treating it like a threat. They're focused on protecting themselves, rather than getting engaged in talking with the audience.

What do you do to protect yourself when you're speaking and feeling afraid? Check the common ones that apply to you and then add your own.

❑ Avoid eye contact with the audience

❑ Talk quickly, to get it over with

❑ Read, rather than speak

❑ Talk in a monotone voice, to keep emotion out of it

❑ Discourage questions

❑ Rely on a colleague

❑ Rely on slides and other visuals in order to reduce your actual speaking time, and distract the audience

_____

_____

_____

_____

_____

_____

Take a moment now to recall the Rule of Opposites—that your gut instinct about what to do in response to a panic attack will be dead wrong, and doing the opposite of your gut instinct will be helpful. You can probably see how it applies to public speaking when you look at the list above. Such responses have the effect of distancing you from your audience. A fearful speaker typically thinks that if he looks at the audience, he'll just get more nervous. He thinks if he makes the talk interesting, or encourages questions, it will just prolong his misery and risk.

But when you detach yourself from the audience in this way, it isolates you at the podium and leaves you all alone with only your fearful thoughts to keep you company. You deprive yourself of contact with the audience at precisely the time when your role as speaker would be much easier if you had a closer connection with the audience. Protecting yourself in this manner makes you more anxious, not less.

You've Been Tricked

If those people were threatening you, it would make sense to protect yourself. "Fight, flight, or freeze" would be helpful. But suppose the audience just wants to hear your information. In that case it wouldn't make sense to protect yourself. Doing so would just make your job harder, and make you feel more nervous.

To work with your anxiety and engage the audience in ways that will reduce, rather than increase, your discomfort, the first thing you can do is to stop trying to hide your nervousness.

One of the most unhelpful suggestions I've ever heard about public speaking is, "Never let 'em see you sweat." You know enough about the Rule of Opposites by now to see what's wrong with this notion. Sweat, visible or invisible, isn't the problem. The real problem is getting uptight about being nervous and thinking it's such a terrible shame and weakness that you have to hide it and keep anybody from noticing it. That leads you to fight against your own uncomfortable emotions, which in turn makes them worse, and . . . you get the idea.

Just remember: fighting, resisting, and hiding your anxiety makes it worse. Admitting, accepting, and working with it makes it better.

Now, does this mean you need to start your presentation with a contrite statement of how afraid you are, and a humble request for their indulgence? No. That would be uncomfortable for everyone. The important thing is to admit to yourself that you're afraid and refrain from pretending otherwise. Lots of people think that they have much more anxiety than anybody else—certainly more than anybody else they know—and that their anxiety is so extreme that they need to hide it, even if others don't. Not true.

The first few minutes of your presentation will probably go better if you can find some way to allude to your anxiety, preferably in a humorous way that fits with your audience and circumstances, rather than to hide it. It's just too much of a burden to try and keep it an absolute secret.

Here are a couple of opening lines that might be appropriate in a variety of business settings:

> "When John asked me to present some material today, I told
> him I hate public speaking, and he comforted me by saying 'Never
> let 'em see you sweat.'" (Cover your armpits in an obvious way.)
> "So, if you'll all close your eyes, I'll get started." Or . . .

Who Says Applause Has to Come Last?

My wife was asked to speak to an audience of several hundred at her church. She dreaded public speaking, but she wanted to do this.

Right at the start, before she said anything else, she told the congregation that she was afraid of public speaking and asked them to pretend that she had already given her talk, that they had really liked it, and it was now time for them to give her a big ovation. And so they did—loudly and boisterously. She thanked them for it and went on with her talk.

She no longer had to worry if they saw she was nervous, because she had already told them she was. She no longer had to worry if they were supportive of her, because they had given her a big round of applause. And she felt no embarrassment, because she had been up front with them in a playful and humorous way. There was no longer anything to hide or protect herself from, so she delivered her talk without incident, and everybody felt good about it.

Her approach probably wouldn't go over as well in a professional or business setting. But you get the general idea. Be open to the possibility of referring to your anxiety in some way that frees you up instead of constricting and controlling you.

"When Jane asked me to present some material today, I told her I was really afraid of public speaking, and she told me to just imagine the audience in their underwear." (Pause and take an obvious look at several rows of people.) "So just give me a minute or so and I'll be ready to start."

With that out of the way, you can turn your attention to the reason you're there—namely, to tell the audience what you've come to tell them. Ideally, you can initiate a conversation with them. These tips will help.

- As you talk, make eye contact with members of the audience. You'll probably find a few people who are particularly attentive, and you can periodically make brief eye contact with them as a way of staying connected to the audience.

- Talk at a comfortable pace. Pause to breathe. Modify your speed to emphasize different points and avoid monotony.

- Check in with the audience periodically to see if they understand your points. Ask them questions, and ask whether they have questions.

- When you find that your focus has drifted to items that are not relevant to your task, such as wondering whether you look anxious, bring it back back to the conversation.

Ten Helpful Hints for Confident Public Speaking

1. Talk, don't perform.

People tend to think of public speaking as requiring an "act," which is different from talking. It doesn't. When you treat public speaking like a performance, you invariably feel more anxious. If you find that you sometimes stumble over your notes, try talking for a few minutes about your topic without notes. You're likely to find yourself more animated, talking without hesitation, and giving a better talk—because it feels "just like talking."

2. Public speaking is you giving the audience a gift.

You have something you're going to give to the audience. You hope they like it and find it useful, interesting, or fun. But what happens after that is up to them. You're just giving them the gift of your knowledge about the topic. Don't try to impress them, show how smart you are, or win their approval. Just give them what you brought for them.

3. Connect with your listeners, rather than distance yourself from them.

People who fear public speaking often distance themselves from the audience because they think if they notice the audience they'll get more afraid. Maybe they will at first. But when you connect with the audience—making eye contact, asking them questions, having them raise their hands to take a quick poll about something—you keep your presentation more in the realm of a conversation, which will feel better and easier as you get used to it.

But if you avoid looking at the audience and read from your notes in a monotone voice at a rapid, fixed rate of speed (or make it "Night of 1000 Slides"), you will lose all contact with your audience. You'll be up there all alone, with only your fearful thoughts of failure to keep you company. You'll feel better if you stay connected.

4. Breathe.

People tend to hold their breath when they're afraid, and then they keep gasping for air as they talk. They feel like they can't stop and catch their breath, because maybe someone will notice that they're nervous. And even if they're willing to stop for air, they often don't know how to do it effectively.

Use the belly-breathing instructions in Chapter 11 to learn how to breathe in a comfortable, relaxed manner. Practice the technique regularly. And when you talk to a group, take the time you need to breathe. One way of doing this is to ask the audience a question and use the interval to get your breathing back on track. But usually all you have to do is pause, catch your breath, and continue. They'll wait.

5. Let your body get into it.

Do you usually talk with your hands? Emphasize your points with gestures? Use your posture and body language to add emphasis and shading to what you're saying? Most people do. So go ahead and do that when you speak to a group as well. Don't stand rigid, feet nailed to the floor, hands clasped, as if you're trying not to fall over. Use your body. Move around. It'll help you feel more natural—just like regular talking.

6. Let your emotions get into it.

People who fear public speaking often struggle to keep emotions out of their talk, lest they succumb to their fear. Find the passion or emotion that you have for your topic, and let it come through as you speak. Let your voice go higher and lower, your volume louder and softer, in concert with the feelings you have for the topic. Don't confine yourself to a monotone voice.

7. Reach out to the audience, don't withdraw into yourself.

If you forget what you were about to say—which happens to even the most seasoned speakers—simply ask the audience, "Where was I?" They'll tell you. Forgot a word you usually know? Ask the audience, "What's the name of that Microsoft browser?" Again, they'll tell you. You don't have to look perfect. Just keeping that in mind can help you relax a lot.

8. Expect and accept anxiety before and during your talk.

A lot of people check in with themselves just before a talk, saying to themselves, "If I feel calm, it'll go well; If I feel really nervous, it'll go badly." Bad idea. It's perfectly normal to feel nervous just before a talk starts. That's usually the peak of your anxiety; expect the nervousness to subside once you get into your talk. Remind yourself that you'll feel better once you get going. It's okay to be afraid, especially at the beginning.

9. Use the powers the listeners have granted to you.

People often feel "trapped" in the role of speaker, like a fly on flypaper: helpless. But the fact is that the audience has granted a lot of power to you. You alone can direct their attention from one topic to another, ask them a question and wait for their answers, ask them to stop and think about a possibility you have just described, ask for a show of hands to poll them on some topic, and so on. They've even agreed to listen to you, rather than others in the audience. You're not trapped—you're in charge.

It will also help you feel more at ease if you make use of whatever else happens during your talk. If someone sneezes, bless them or say *gesundheit*. If your voice cracks, make a joke about your voice changing. Whatever happens, don't ignore it—use it.

10. Have reasonable expectations of the audience.

In general, audiences want you to succeed and do well, because it will be more enjoyable and informative for them. So be sure to monitor your thoughts about the audience, and be skeptical of any concerns that the audience is "out to get you," hopes to see you fall apart, or is thoroughly turned off by your talk. Even when a talk is going well, speakers tend to notice particular signs, such as someone yawning or leaving early, and think of them as negative evaluations. These thoughts are usually just symptoms of anxiety, not an accurate reading of the audience reaction.

Since you're talking to a group, there will probably be a variety of reactions, and it will be helpful to allow for them. Some people may yawn—whether because they're bored or more likely because they haven't been getting enough sleep lately. Other people may leave early or have furtive conversations. You won't usually have an opportunity to ask why during your talk, so allow audience members to have a variety of reactions, recognizing that different people have different circumstances.

21

....

Driving

One of the most disabling phobias associated with panic attacks is the fear of driving. In many areas, driving is a daily necessity, and your life can be severely restricted by limitations such as where, when, or how you can drive.

The fact that you panic while driving a powerful vehicle that weighs a ton or more may seem like a particularly difficult problem to solve. In other panic situations, the panic sufferer plays a relatively passive role—a passenger on a train, a shopper in a store, a worshipper at church, a person getting a haircut—when they experience a panic attack. Their main task is to ride it out until it passes, or until they have left the scene. But drivers cannot remain entirely passive. They have to continue to operate the vehicle, at least for a while. People who experience panic attacks while driving, particularly on high-speed roads, fear not only losing control of themselves but also losing control of the vehicle.

People usually assume that they are "out of control" during panic attacks and therefore that they will be unable to drive safely during one. If you actually drive in a dangerous and erratic manner during a panic attack, this problem needs to be taken seriously and resolved. But keep in mind that panic often fools you into believing things that simply aren't true. Don't take your fearful assumptions as the truth. Instead, use the materials in this chapter to review your actual driving behavior and determine whether you can drive safely during a panic attack.

Let's start by considering the nature of the fear you experience. Simply calling it a driving phobia makes it sound like your fear prevents you from driving, even though you know how to drive and are licensed to do so. That happens to some people, but for the great majority it's more complicated than that. It's much more common for people to impose limits on their driving in response to their fears. For instance, a lot of people who come to me for help with a driving phobia do drive but avoid expressways or other specific circumstances such as overpasses and bridges.

Part of avoiding expressway driving may involve the higher speeds on those roads. But what can be more upsetting is the fact there are only certain points at which one can exit the expressway. A road sign that says "Next Exit—12 Miles" might as well say "Next Panic Attack—1 Mile!" As soon as someone starts worrying "What if I have a panic attack when the exit is still 11 miles away?" the next thing they know, they're having a full-blown attack.

The same person might be able to take an alternate route, a local road with lots of intersections, and drive 30 miles without breaking a sweat. What makes the difference? It's not necessarily how far they drive, or how fast. It's the thought of being "trapped" on the road without an exit nearby. It's the thought of having a panic attack with no way to get off the expressway. The thought of being trapped can also lead people to avoid bridges, tunnels, overpasses, left turn lanes, red lights, ferry boats, the center or left lanes of multilane roads, roads under construction, or roads without a shoulder.

It will help to carefully review the details of your driving phobia. Let's start by taking an inventory of the limits you impose on your driving.

In the past year, have you driven a car at all?   ❑ Yes   ❑ No
(If your answer is "no," move on to the bottom of page 215.)

On the following list, check the driving conditions you prefer to avoid. If you absolutely never drive on expressways, for instance, check the "Always Avoid" column. If you usually avoid such driving but sometimes do it, check the "Avoid with Exceptions" column. If you don't avoid a particular road condition at all, make no marks for that item. **Then add any others that aren't on the list.**

DRIVING CONDITION	ALWAYS AVOID	AVOID WITH EXCEPTIONS
Expressways with limited access	❑	❑
Roads through areas with no homes or stores where you can stop	❑	❑
Roads where the speed limit is 50 mph or greater	❑	❑
Red lights	❑	❑
Left turn lanes at busy intersections	❑	❑
Busy roads at rush hour	❑	❑
Express lanes	❑	❑

DRIVING CONDITION	ALWAYS AVOID	AVOID WITH EXCEPTIONS
Roads without shoulders	❏	❏
Roads under construction	❏	❏
Driving in the middle lane	❏	❏
Driving in the left lane	❏	❏
Unfamiliar roads	❏	❏
Bridges	❏	❏
Tunnels	❏	❏
Car washes	❏	❏
Driving at night	❏	❏
Emission testing stations	❏	❏
others _____	❏	❏
_____		
_____	❏	❏
_____		
_____	❏	❏
_____		
_____	❏	❏
_____		
_____	❏	❏
_____		
_____	❏	❏
_____		
_____	❏	❏
_____		
_____	❏	❏
_____		

Now look at the "Avoid with Exceptions" column and consider the times when you drive in circumstances you normally avoid. Think about the reason you can, at least sometimes, drive in those circumstances. It's probably not random. There are probably some rules that tell you whether or not today is a day when you can drive in one of these situations.

What makes it possible for you to sometimes drive in these situations?

DRIVING CONDITION

_____

Recent exception   Reason

_____   _____

_____   _____

DRIVING CONDITION

_____

Recent exception   Reason

_____   _____

_____   _____

DRIVING CONDITION

_____

Recent exception   Reason

_____   _____

_____   _____

DRIVING CONDITION

_____

Recent exception   Reason

_____   _____

_____   _____

DRIVING CONDITION

_____

Recent exception   Reason

_____   _____

_____   _____

Common reasons for exceptions include the following:

- *Dire Need.* For example, having to take a child to a doctor's appointment when no one else is available to drive may require that you pass through an area you usually avoid or go beyond your "safe zone."

- *Upbeat, Optimistic Mood.* On days when you feel especially good, for whatever reason, you feel capable of more than on days when you don't feel so good.

- *Support People.* If you have your "support person" with you, you probably do more than you can without him or her, even though you do all the driving.

- *Support Objects.* When you have certain objects with you, like a cellular phone or a water bottle, you may do more than when you don't have them.

- *Good Days/Bad Days.* You may have some general rules that you don't think of too often but that influence your choices. Often they involve some kind of association with a particularly bad attack you've had. If you had a bad attack on a Monday, or in early December, you might subconsciously lay low at those times and not "push your luck."

- *Hospital Locations.* Knowing where the nearest hospital is frequently makes a difference to people with panic attacks. The reassurance of knowing that a hospital is just down the road can enable them to drive through an area which they might otherwise avoid.

- *Distraction.* Listening to a favorite tape or CD, chatting with a good friend on the phone, or engaging in some other distracting task often helps people to travel further than they would otherwise.

- *Weather.* For many people, pleasant weather seems to make driving more possible.

What are you afraid will happen if you have a panic attack while driving?
If you're having trouble with this question, recall a specific major panic attack you had while driving. Imagine that I was in the car with you and at the height of the attack, I asked you "What are you afraid is going to happen now?"

_____

_____

_____

_____

_____

_____

Yes, you'll get afraid, but the question is, what will be the *result* of the attack? What is the worst outcome you fear as a result of having a panic attack while driving? A lot of people don't get to the bottom of their fear when they first try to answer this. They may identify some symptoms they'd experience. For instance, they might say, "I'd hyperventilate" or "I'd have to pull onto the shoulder and stop driving." Then my follow-up question would be, "And if you do, what's the worst thing that will happen as a result of that?" They might say "People will see me stopped there and wonder what's wrong with me," and again I'd have to ask, "And what would be the worst consequence if they did?"

Review your own answers and make sure you get to the bottom line. What would the worst outcome be?

Once you have that answer, move on to the following questions.

In the past, what has been the worst result of having a panic attack while driving? How did it compare to what you feared?

_____

_____

_____

_____

_____

If you have special exceptions that allow you to occasionally drive beyond your boundaries, how do they work? Do they help make you safer or more calm?

_____

_____

_____

_____

_____

_____

When you panic while driving, what do you do to help yourself?

_____

_____

_____

_____

And how do those things work? Do they make you safer or more calm?

_____

_____

_____

_____

_____

_____

If your panic attacks while driving didn't produce any dangerous or catastrophic outcomes, how do you explain that?

_____

_____

_____

_____

_____

_____

With respect to the first question—what you fear will be the outcome of having a panic attack while driving—many people identify one or some of the following:

- Die, faint, or go crazy
- Cause a crash by suddenly slamming on the brakes, or jumping across lanes of traffic without warning
- Abandon the car and flee in some dangerous fashion
- Become so paralyzed with fear that they are unable to function
- Stall out the car and be unable to get it moving again
- Have a heart attack or a psychotic episode while stranded in traffic amid hundreds of angry motorists honking at them.

Reviewing your answers to the rest of the questions above may help you to realize that:

1. _Panic does not produce the dangerous or catastrophic outcomes you fear._ In fact, I know of only one client in more than 20 years who has had an accident of any kind during a panic attack—she clipped the side of her garage. People can experience a lot of fear

and still do an adequate, safe job of driving. The results of panic attacks are all about discomfort, not danger.

2. *All special exceptions that allow people to occasionally drive when they would normally avoid it seem to work by influencing the person's mood or comfort level or need to drive,* not by making their driving any safer.

3. *People try to help themselves during a panic attack while driving in a variety of ways,* including singing, yelling, praying, opening the windows, turning on the air conditioner, pinching and slapping themselves, turning the radio on, turning the radio off, eating snacks, playing with their hair, calling friends on their cellular phones, and pulling off the road. Of all these efforts, only pulling off the road has the slightest possible connection to making them safer. All the others are purely devoted to distraction and comfort. Even those who do pull off the road typically do so to regain their composure and then resume driving. They don't abandon their car, nor do they call friends, towing services, or the state police to come get them.

4. *In the throes of a panic attack, you still remain in control of your actions.* People tend to attribute the fact that they didn't get into a terrible accident, or abandon their car and run across six lanes of traffic, to luck, distraction, support people, support objects, and the various efforts they made. But upon closer examination of those factors, you can probably see that while they may make a person more comfortable, they don't make a person safe. They don't protect against insanity, heart attacks, or collisions. The real explanation is that panic doesn't lead to dangerous or catastrophic outcomes because that's not the nature of panic.

What about Distracting Yourself?

Distraction can sometimes ease problems of discomfort, and that's why people reach for it. The fact that you use distraction can be a helpful reminder of what you're up against. Would you distract yourself if you were really in danger? If you saw a big truck barreling out of control toward you, would you hum a little tune, or would you steer out of the way?

People instinctively reach for distraction when they face discomfort, but not danger.

That's what happens during a panic attack. You're feeling afraid, upset, and miserable, and you need to relax. But you *can* drive when you're feeling afraid, upset, and miserable, just as you can drive when you're sad, glad, angry, jealous, lonely, or hopeful. You can drive with a wide variety of emotions.

When a person is having a panic attack, they experience such powerful emotions and physical sensations that it can feel as though they're losing control of themselves somehow. This is the panic trick. They feel so upset, so "out of control," that they assume they *are* out of control. But feelings and thoughts aren't the way to tell if you're acting responsibly and "in control." The best evidence about whether you're in control is what you're doing.

In the case of a panic attack while driving, especially on expressways, people tend to assume that they are out of control and will therefore lose control of the vehicle, and cause a terrible accident. That's an understandable fear. You feel powerfully afraid during a panic attack, and it seems to make sense that you might lose control of your car.

If that's still how it seems to you, I have a couple more questions.

Do you have a history of traffic violations and/or accidents that were the result of panic attacks?

_____

If I were a state patrolman, following a couple of car lengths behind you, would I notice anything about your driving that would lead me to pull you over and maybe have you walk a straight line or give you a ticket?

_____

If your answer to either of these questions is "yes," you need to address that aspect of your driving. If you actually drive in a reckless or lawless fashion, that's a good reason to limit your driving until you get that problem resolved.

But most people answer "no" to both questions. They haven't had tickets or accidents as a result of panic. They report nothing that a patrolman would notice. In fact, they drive carefully. They stay within their lanes. They use their turn signals and mirrors when changing lanes. They usually don't drive any faster than the traffic around them (although speeding is the one violation that comes up occasionally). They'll sometimes attribute their good driving record to luck or other circumstances, but when they examine their actual behavior, they find no examples of being out of control. That's the test. Control is about behavior, not thoughts or emotions. If you have a reasonably clean record, that's a strong indication that you're up against discomfort, not danger.

Progressive Exposure and Driving

If, after you review your driving history, you find that your driving passes the test of being reasonable and safe, it makes sense to develop a program of progressive exposure as outlined in Chapter 18. Develop a hierarchy of driving tasks, as described in that chapter, and practice regularly with those tasks, using the AWARE steps to help guide you through the panic when it comes.

Here's how one individual I know—let's call him Joe—used the AWARE steps to guide himself through a panic attack during his driving exposure:

- *Acknowledge & Accept*: Joe talked to himself about the fact that he was having a panic attack, and how he was reacting to it. "Looks like I'm finally having a panic attack. I wish I wasn't, and I'm not grateful for the chance to practice. I just want to get to my sales call. I'm tired of this $#!%. But if this is what has to happen now, while I'm driving to my meeting, so be it. Bring it on. I'm not going to pretend it's not happening, or pretend I don't notice. Not asking God to help. It's a pain in the ass, but so what. I'll just keep going, it'll pass sooner or later."

- *Wait & Watch*: Joe reminded himself of his options, such as pulling over onto the shoulder and waiting it out or putting on his hazard lights and driving more slowly, and decided he didn't need to use those options right then. He decided to keep them in mind if he felt worse; in the meantime he would keep driving. He "watched" by switching on a tape recorder and talking out his panic diary answers.

- *Actions to increase comfort*: Joe switched into belly breathing. He checked himself to see what parts of his body were particularly tense and stiff. He noticed he was holding the steering wheel in a death grip and relaxed his hands. He noticed his arms were rigidly extended, and he relaxed those muscles as well, getting a bend in his elbows and allowing for a lighter grip on the wheel. He noticed his hands were sweaty, and he wiped them. He rolled down the window to get some fresh air. He found that he was keeping his vision locked straight ahead, so he started glancing around, looking at other traffic and sights along the way. He checked his reflection in the rearview mirror to see if he looked like a crazy person and satisfied himself that he looked like his usual self.

- *Repeat*: Joe went through this cycle four times during a 35-minute ride and frequently reminded himself that this attack would . . .

- *End*. And so it did. (It will for you, too.)

A Final Suggestion: "Dress Rehearsals"

Before you get very far with your exposure situations, practice pulling off the road a few times. The key to realizing that you're not "trapped" is knowing you have options you can use. One of the best options, if you feel unable to drive safely or just need a break, is to pull over and compose yourself, or even wait for help if necessary.

People with panic attacks often fear pulling over because they have a heckling thought like "What if I can't get back on the road?" If you wait until you're actually having a panic attack to pull onto the shoulder for the first time, it will be harder to exercise this option. So do some "dress rehearsals." Pull over *as if* you were having a panic attack and rehearse the AWARE steps you'd go through if you were actually experiencing panic. Go through each step—do your breathing, fill out a diary, and so on. Do this several times, on all the road types that appear on your hierarchy. That way, when you do experience a panic attack and worry about being "trapped," you'll be able to remind yourself that you've already had the experience of pulling over, and you just need to do the same thing again.

22
....

Claustrophobia

Claustrophobia is usually defined as the fear of being confined in a small space. Elevators and flying are the most common reasons people seek help with claustrophobia, but some people have other claustrophobic concerns, such as MRI procedures or small workspaces.

People usually think of claustrophobia as being limited to small spaces, but size is relative. The usable space inside most commercial jets offers more walking room than many urban apartments, but few people report claustrophobia inside their home—unless they're confined indoors by a heavy snowfall or a holiday visit from their in-laws.

And that offers a hint about the other key factor in claustrophobia—*control*. Claustrophobia isn't simply about the size of the space but also about how much control you have, or think you have, over the situation. Even though an airplane isn't terribly small, claustrophobic people focus on the fact that they can't leave an airplane in midflight and the possibility that they'll be confined to their seats by turbulence. The size of the space is an important factor, but so is control over your coming and going.

I think it's helpful—and reasonably accurate—to think of most claustrophobia as a special case of panic disorder. People fear being confined in small spaces because they worry about having a panic attack where a quick exit may be difficult or impossible because of space restrictions. Almost anything can seem like a "trap" if you're having a panic attack, but with claustrophobia, the cue is always a physical restriction on your ability to leave.

When I first started working with patients who feared elevators, even though I applied the same cognitive behavioral methods that had proven successful with other panic phobias, the results were disappointing. Reviewing my treatment failures revealed the reason. When one of those first clients went out to ride an elevator with me, they invariably wanted to take a short ride—usually just one floor to start with—*and then get off the elevator* to calm down. I naïvely agreed to this out of concern that they wouldn't ride at all unless I let them get out frequently. But the result was that they never calmed down while riding the elevator. They only got relief when they stepped off. This had the unfortunate effect of maintaining and strengthening their fear. While riding in the car, they struggled against the fear, trying to keep their composure as they waited for their next chance to step outside the car. This strengthened their habitual, fearful responses and didn't allow them to become desensitized to the fear.

Once I realized this, I started asking clients to spend the entire exposure session in the elevator without stepping out, and the results improved dramatically. Resigning themselves to staying in the elevator for an extended period of time, people gave up their resistance to the fear and therefore became desensitized in a much shorter time.

This highlights a key aspect of elevator phobia that can block your recovery. The ride is typically so short that there's a natural temptation to just "tough it out" and get to your destination. This makes the particular ride possible, but it does not contribute to your recovery from the fear. You need to stay on the elevator long enough for the fear to "peak and pass."

Some therapists take a different approach, distracting the elevator phobic while they ride together. For instance, as soon as the door closes, they may drop a jarful of pennies on the floor and direct the client to pick them up while riding the elevator to the top floor and back. But in my experience, this provides exactly the wrong lesson, reinforcing the idea that the individual has to *get away* from the fear somehow. It may help convince them that they can get away from the anxiety with such distracting methods, but it fails to address the immediate source of the panic—their own resistance and struggle against it. Until you practice *giving in* to the fear, you won't find out how giving in allows it to subside.

The Claustrophobe's Car

One claustrophobic client of mine had reached the stage in his treatment when the next step was to go out and practice with elevators in nearby office buildings. He mentioned that he would like to drive (no surprise there), so we took his car. What *did* surprise me was the discovery that he drove an extremely tiny car. I'm just slightly under six feet tall, and I had to keep my head slightly bowed, as if in church, to avoid smacking my head against the roof.

I pointed out the irony of a person with claustrophobia owning such a small car. He grinned and replied, "Yes, but I'm at the wheel!" That, of course, was the most important factor for him.

Tower of Terror

One of my claustrophobic clients related to me her experience with a so-called "amusement ride" called the Tower of Terror in a Florida theme park. This scary ride takes passengers up and down three times in an all-too-real simulation of an elevator gone wildly out of control. During the first ascent and drop, she felt so terrified that she feared she was about to die and said so to her sister who was riding with her. The sister told her they had two more up-and-down trips to go. On learning this, my client gave up and accepted what she believed was her imminent death, saying to herself, "This is it, then . . ." Immediately upon giving in to the idea that she would die, her panic subsided, and she completed the ride without further panic.

Hard as it is to believe, what maintains the panic is struggling against it. Giving in to the panic, as she did, deprives it of energy, much as enclosing a burning candle in an airtight jar deprives it of the oxygen it needs to keep burning. Because of this, a recovery based on getting away from the anxiety is far less reliable and long-lasting than one based on the realization that you can feel the anxiety, give in to it, let it pass, and life goes on as before.

The Tower of Terror experience also demonstrates once again that our gut instincts about how to handle panic and fear are usually wrong, and that progress comes when we are willing to do the opposite. It turned out to be a good reminder for my client, who could then use it to remind herself to give in to panic attacks instead of resisting them.

The exercises that follow pertain to one of the most common claustrophobic fear, elevators. (The other most common one, fear of flying, is covered in an earlier chapter.) If your claustrophobic fear pertains to some other kind of situation, the same general principles apply; modify these exercises to suit your own situation.

Which of the following describes the most you're presently able to do with elevators?

❑ Think about riding an elevator

❑ Stand in the lobby and look at one

❑ Step into an elevator while keeping the door open

❑ Stand in an elevator with the door closed, but not allowing it to move

❑ Ride in an elevator

For the activity you checked above, what symptoms do you experience in each of these four categories?

Physical Sensations _____

_____

_____

_____

_____

Thoughts _____

_____

_____

_____

_____

Emotions _____

_____

_____

_____

_____

Behaviors_____

_____

_____

_____

_____

If you are unable to avoid or leave the situation, what do you do to try and help yourself?

_____

_____

_____

_____

_____

People often stare at the buttons as they illuminate to monitor the elevator's progress, stand in front of the controls so no one else can touch the buttons for fear they'll harm the machinery, stand very still so as not to rock or otherwise disturb the elevator, hold onto the walls of the elevator or lean against the walls, or try to distract themselves from the fact that they are riding in an elevator.

What circumstances change the level of fear you experience or expect?

_____

_____

_____

_____

_____

For instance, you may feel less anxious if you ride an elevator with a trusted friend, or if the elevator is empty or uncrowded. Other factors that often make a difference include dark versus brightly lit, slow versus fast, self-service versus human-operated, glass versus opaque, noisy versus quiet, and old versus new.

What do you fear will happen to you if you ride in an elevator?

_____

_____

_____

_____

_____

As you identify your fear, ask yourself, "And if that happens, what am I afraid will be the result?" until you reach your bottom line, ultimate fear. For instance, if you fear that the elevator will get stuck, what are you afraid will happen next as a result of the elevator getting stuck? If you're afraid that people will see you get upset, cry, or hyperventilate, what do you fear will happen as a result of that unpleasant experience? In short, what is the worst outcome you fear?

What is the worst thing that ever happened to you on an elevator?

_____

_____

_____

_____

_____

After answering these questions, put them aside and return to them a day or two later, to revise and expand upon your answers. In the meantime, go visit an elevator, even if you're not prepared to step inside it. At least visit the lobby area and take note of your reactions, looking for additional details with which to answer the questions. When you're done, you should have more information about your fear than you have ever considered before. This will probably enable you to step a little more into the "observer" role and out of the "victim" role.

Now you are ready to design your exposure practice. The first step is to select one or two elevators for your first practice sessions. Visit a variety of buildings with elevators and see how each rates with your criteria. Select an elevator you are willing to start with. It doesn't have to be the scariest, or even rank high on your list. It's okay to start with the "easiest" one.

Decide whether you're going to do this solo or with a support person. Be aware that the presence of such a person is a mixed blessing at best. If you are able to do the exposure on your own, without a support person, that will actually help you to progress faster. But if you're unwilling or unable to approach an elevator ride alone, you'll be better off starting with one, and getting them out of the picture as soon as possible. Explain carefully what you want your support person to do. Review our earlier discussions of self disclosure and working with a support person so that you can communicate effectively about your problem. Besides the general guidelines set forth there, give your support person the following information specific to elevators:

- *Tell your support person that you will make all the decisions.* You will be in charge, and they will just accompany you. You will decide when to ride, where to ride, whether they should ride with you or wait for you, and so on.

- *Tell your support person that you'll probably get afraid and have all kinds of unpleasant feelings.* Maybe you'll look pale and frightened. Maybe you'll cry. That's okay. Tell them not to "rescue" you, that these feelings are only discomfort, not danger. If you cry, they can offer you a tissue, nothing more. Remind them that you're riding on the elevator to practice dealing with your fear, so you're supposed to get afraid.

- *Have a plan about what to say in the unlikely event that someone asks what you're doing.* If you reach the top or bottom floor and find people waiting to let you out before they board the elevator, tell them "I'm just riding," and let it go at that. If someone were to ask more of an explanation, you could simply tell them you're working on a fear of elevators. But from my experience, they won't ask.

228 PANIC ATTACKS WORKBOOK

- *Tell your support person what you want them to do.* For instance, they can help with reminders that you have a plan to follow ("Are you doing your breathing?" "Is there anything you want me to do?") and encourage you to stay with it and get good practice with fear. If they see you doing something avoidant or unhelpful, they can ask you about it (but leave the response up to you).

Here are some exposure guidelines to follow while riding the elevator:

1. Start with small steps. Move on to the next step as soon as you are willing.

2. Most people want to start the riding phase by riding up one flight, then getting out to calm down. If you are willing, skip this stage and you will progress more quickly because it is ideal to ride continuously, without getting out of the elevator, until it becomes boring.

3. If you are not ready to start riding continuously, start with what you're willing to do, but the sooner you move to continuous riding, the easier it will go for you.

4. Choose long-term freedom, not immediate comfort.

5. Be sure to abstain from your "coping steps and support objects." In particular, don't hold on or lean against the walls.

6. Breathe.

7. Use the AWARE steps.

8. Take notes using the panic diary.

23

....

Social Phobia

Social phobia differs slightly from other panic-inducing phobias because it involves fears of humiliation and shame, rather than death or insanity. But the intensity of the fear, and the demoralization the sufferer experiences, are just as difficult to manage. Their responses are likely to involve social withdrawal and avoidance. If you have social phobia, you can use all the methods I have described in this book to help you overcome this problem. The only modifications you need to make are a matter of emphasis.

Social phobia is remarkably similar to panic disorder in the way the fear "works" and the way people respond to it. Only the specific fear is different. People with social phobia fear that they will act foolishly or show their nervousness in front of others in degrading ways. They worry about what others will think of them, not what will happen to them

This difference in feared outcome leads to other differences. People with social phobia tend to put greater emphasis on visible symptoms of panic, such as blushing and sweating. They often worry more about perspiration appearing on their face than their underarms, because it is more visible there. For people with panic disorder, the main concern about these symptoms is their worry that maybe the blushing or sweating is a sign of a heart attack. But if you have social phobia, the fear is that others will notice these symptoms and think you odd or peculiar. Moreover, a person with social phobia worries that if others notice these symptoms, he or she will attract more attention and thereby make the sweating and/or blushing all the worse.

People with social phobia and panic disorder go through the same vicious cycle of expecting and anticipating trouble, and then seeking to protect themselves from that trouble by avoidance and various means of self-protection. In both cases, their efforts to protect themselves are actually the main problem. In both cases, they get "tricked" into trying to protect themselves in ways that make their troubles worse and more long-lasting, instead of better.

If you have social phobia, your efforts to protect yourself from humiliation not only limit your social activities but also maintain your fears and block you from the actions that would reduce them. To illustrate this point, let's consider the experience of a person with social phobia—let's call him Tom—who decides to attend a party.

Tom, naturally, has been wrestling with anticipatory anxiety about the party since he received the invitation. He delayed accepting the invitation as long as possible, but this delay served to increase his anxiety, not decrease it, since he reviewed the decision every day while delaying his reply. He worried about drawing negative attention to himself in various ways—"freezing up" and not having anything to say when spoken to, looking obviously anxious due to sweating and blushing, saying something foolish or rude, or clumsily dropping glasses and silverware in ways that draw attention to him.

Accepting the invitation did not reduce his anxiety level, because he continued to entertain the possibility of canceling with a last minute excuse. Right up to the point when Tom knocked on the door, he was debating whether or not to go through with it, and this debate naturally increased his anxiety level.

Tom's anxiety basically stemmed from the fact that he believed he would be quite nervous at the party, based on past experience, and he also believed that this was a terrible and shameful thing. He believed that he should find some way to not be nervous, or at least to not let anyone notice his nervousness, so most of his worrying was about being "found out" as a nervous person. From past experience, he expected to have the following symptoms at the party:

Physical Sensations:
- Blushing
- Heart racing
- Trembling voice
- Sweating
- Gasping for air

Emotions:
- Fear
- Embarrassment
- Shame

Thoughts:

- I don't fit in, and look really odd to them
- They feel sorry for me, but wouldn't want to get to know me
- I better keep my distance, lest they find out how anxious I am
- Don't let them see how uncomfortable I am

Behaviors:

- Stands apart from the group
- Listens, doesn't talk
- Responds with one-word answers or with questions designed to get others talking so he can be silent again
- Suppresses his own opinions
- Tries so hard to avoid attention and controversy that he makes himself seem dull
- Arrives early, maybe helps set up, and leaves early
- Wears a turtleneck, combs hair in his face, and stays in dimmest parts of the room in an effort to hide blushing
- Focuses on himself, not the people around him, in an effort to monitor his symptoms, for example, monitors himself for warm feelings that would indicate blushing and frequently touches his face to monitor for sweating.

Tom's underlying belief is that he has significant weaknesses and deficiencies that make him quite different from other people, and he is afraid that others will discover this. He believes that if they did, at least two terrible things would happen. He would receive unfavorable attention, which would make him more nervous in the moment, perhaps to the point of acting in some bizarre manner or having some kind of a breakdown. And he would be the subject of scorn and disregard, even if everyone hid their reactions from him.

Tom has no history of actually behaving inappropriately or receiving hostile attention from others. But he assumes that he knows what others are thinking, so he continues to believe in his viewpoint without any actual proof.

The most "vicious" part of this cycle is that Tom consistently tries to protect himself from these feared outcomes by using the same behaviors. This strengthens and maintains his fears in at least two ways.

First, it prevents him from testing out his predictions of humiliation and rejection. He is thus likely to go through his entire life being "fooled" by fears that are unrealistic and exaggerated. If he succeeds, for instance, in never letting anyone see that he is nervous, he never gets to find out what actually happens to him if they do. He can continue to believe it would be a tragedy, when it would proba-bly be nothing more than a passing episode of embarrassment. It might even be a good thing; he might find out others were nervous as well. But his drive to pro-tect himself keeps him stuck.

Second, his focus during the party is on monitoring himself instead of inter-acting with others. If someone were trying to attract his attention in an effort to get to know him, he might not even notice, because he'd be so preoccupied with monitoring his sweat glands. And, of course, the more you think about sweat, the more likely you are to notice some, or even produce some. So Tom goes to the party with the intention, not of socializing with others, but of somehow "getting through" the event without disgracing himself.

By making this his goal, the best he can hope for is a dull evening in which nothing of any interest happens.

Does any of this describe what you do and think? If so, what are some of the ways you "protect" yourself in social situations?

_____

_____

_____

_____

_____

_____

What are some of the ways you monitor yourself for signs of anxiety in social situations?

_____

_____

_____

_____

_____

Does anybody in your life know about your social anxiety? If yes, who?

_____

_____

_____

Do you periodically discuss your social anxiety with that person? If so, how does talking about it affect how you feel?

_____

_____

_____

Have you ever had the unexpected occasion to talk about your social anxiety with someone? If so, what was the result?

_____

_____

_____

If you're like most people with social phobia, you get some relief from talking about it. It doesn't produce the terrible outcomes you associate with revealing your anxiety—quite the opposite. The worst of these feelings comes from hiding and resisting your social anxiety, not disclosing it.

If that reminds you of the Rule of Opposites, it should. All the "tricks" I've described in this book apply to social phobia as well. The way out of social phobia is the same as the way out of panic disorder. Identify the ways in which you have been tricked into doing what maintains your fears—and begin experimenting with the opposite.

It's easy to get fooled into thinking you know what others are thinking (or would be thinking if they knew you were so nervous). The truth is, you don't know what they're thinking at all. You know what _you're_ thinking, and you project that onto them. You're like the cartoonist who puts thoughts in the heads of his characters—but they're still his thoughts, not theirs. Begin to treat these thoughts like the heckling thoughts we discussed in Chapter 17, not as if they were accurate, important predictions.

You get fooled into focusing on yourself, your thoughts and sensations, when you would do better to focus on the people around you and get involved with them. Focusing on others will increase your discomfort at the beginning, of course, but if you stay with it, you'll actually get so interested in them that you begin to let go of some of your self-monitoring, and this will reduce your anxiety.

Expect, acknowledge, and accept your fear. Don't stand on guard duty watching for it. You get fooled into isolating yourself, hiding yourself from others in an effort to protect yourself from the anxiety, when you would actually do more to free yourself from anxiety by giving up the protection.

Involve yourself in the present moment, rather than the "what if" future you can imagine.

A number of resources for people with social phobia are listed in the back of this book—and you should take a look at them. Let me emphasize one central point about social phobia and I urge you to keep it in mind as you review and use other resources that are available: You don't overcome social phobia by first learning how to quell your anxiety before going out into social situations. You overcome this phobia, like all other phobias, by going out to accept and practice with the anxiety. The path to progress starts with accepting your anxiety and becoming more active.

The best way around anxiety is right through it.

....

Postscript

I hope you've found this workbook interesting, relevant, and most of all, helpful. I hope it helps you break the trick of panic attacks and phobias.

People typically approach these methods wondering whether they will "cure" them. That's not the word I like to use. It implies that panic is a disease and that once you've been vaccinated, it's impossible for you to catch it again.

Panic is much more like a trick than a disease. It's a trick that takes ordinary anxiety and other normal self-protective responses and blows them out of proportion until you can barely recognize them for what they are.

You can use the methods in this book to handle panic so well that you lose your fear of it. When you do, it fades away. You can recover your freedom to do whatever you want and go wherever you want, undeterred by panic or the anticipation of panic. You can make a great recovery, and put panic and phobias out of your life.

But you'll still have the ordinary anxiety that's a part of the human condition. And naturally there will be times in your life when your anxiety level goes up and down. I prefer to use the term "recovery" instead of "cure." If you think you're cured and then go through a stressful time of life with heightened anxiety, you're liable to start worrying about the strength of your "cure," and worry that your "disease" is coming back. Think of it as a recovery, in the same sense that Alcoholics Anonymous uses it. There, you can meet men and women who haven't had a drink in more than 20 years. They won't tell you they're cured. They'll tell you they're recovering alcoholics. Think of yourself as a recovering phobic.

Will you have trouble with panic or anxiety during your recovery? It's possible. If you go through a turbulent time in the future, it's only natural that you'll feel something. If you do, pull out this workbook again. Go down in the basement and find your notes. Refresh your memory about the panic trick, the belly breathing, and the Rule of Opposites. Dust off the habits that helped you recover.

That's all you need.

....

Resources

Books

Brown, Duane. 1996. *Flying Without Fear.* Oakland, CA: New Harbinger Publications, Inc.

Butler, Gillian. 1999. *Overcoming Social Anxiety and Shyness: A Self-Help Guide Using Cognitive Behavioral Techniques.* London: Robinson Publishing.

Burns, David. 1989. *The Feeling Good Handbook.* New York: Penguin Books.

Desberg, Peter. 1996. *No More Butterflies: Overcoming Stagefright, Shyness, Interview Anxiety, & Fear of Public Speaking.* Oakland, CA: New Harbinger Publications.

Greenberger, Dennis, & Padesky, Christine, 1995. *Mind Over Mood.* New York: Guilford Press.

Markway, Carmin, Pollard, & Flynn. 1992. *Dying of Embarrassment: Help for Social Anxiety & Phobia.* Oakland, CA: New Harbinger Publications.

Roland, David. 1997. *The Confident Performer.* Portsmouth, New Hampshire: Heinemann.

Tomaro, Ph.D., Michael 2000. *Flying in the Comfort Zone.* Milwaukee, Wisconsin: Institute for Human Factors.

Weekes, Claire. 1969. *Hope and Health for Your Nerves.* New York: Bantam Books.

———. 1972. *Peace from Nervous Suffering.* New York: Bantam Books.

Wilson, Reid. 1987. *Don't Panic: Taking Control of Anxiety Attacks.* New York: Harper & Row.

Internet

<www.anxietycoach.com> Dr. David Carbonell's self-help site
<www.adaa.org> Anxiety Disorders Association of America
<www.anxieties.com> Dr. Reid Wilson's self-help site

<www.algy.com/anxiety/index.shtml> The anxiety panic internet
   resource (TAPIR)

<www.toastmasters.org> Toastmasters International

The following organizations offer a free "Find a Therapist" service on their websites.

<www.adaa.org> Anxiety Disorders Association of America

<www.abct.org> Association for Behavioral and Cognitive Therapies

Support Groups

The help you get in a support group comes from yourself and the relationship you establish with the group. The group doesn't offer treatment, but provides a forum in which you can discuss your efforts, get feedback and encouragement, and feel less alone. The expertise of the group typically comes from the members' personal experiences and struggles with anxiety problems, rather than from professional training.

I've seen excellent groups that helped a lot of people, average groups that provided some helpful contact among members but little else, and harmful groups that encouraged people to follow practices that unfortunately maintained, rather than relieved, phobic patterns. All were well intentioned, but some groups take on a "protectionist" stance that discourages people from working with the kinds of exposure methods I discuss in this book, methods that are the core of cognitive behavioral approaches to panic.

When considering a support group, be an informed consumer. No group will be everything to every person. Take the good they have to offer, and leave the rest. Some of the important qualities of a good support group are:

- All members should share a common problem, the more specific the better. "Mental health" is too broad. It should at least be restricted to "Anxiety," and preferably to "Panic/Phobias."
- The group should value educational resources, offer information about such resources, and encourage their use.
- The group should promote a goal-oriented approach and encourage members to discuss their specific goals each week if they wish.
- The group should allow members to listen for a brief introductory period without talking, if they wish.
- The group should not permit members to use their group time simply to complain or deplore their helplessness.
- The group should maintain an open mind toward the treatment choices of its members, and should not attempt to replace professional treatment.
- The group should be run for the benefit of members, not as a source of clients for a particular therapist or agency.

- What is said in the group should stay there and never be repeated elsewhere. Confidentiality should be protected and respected.
- The group should maintain an "open door" policy that makes it easy for people to join or leave it.
- Only one person should talk at a time.
- Fees should be low and should exist only to support the cost of group meetings and educational materials.
- The group should be reasonably able to resolve disputes and sources of internal friction.

To locate a support group in your community:

Check with the **Anxiety Disorders Association of America**. This is a national nonprofit group devoted to education, treatment, and research on behalf of people with anxiety disorders. They have a list of support groups, state by state, on their website. They also have materials and suggestions for people who want to start a support group in their community.

8730 Georgia Avenue, Suite 600

Silver Spring, MD 20910

240-485-1001

www.adaa.org

Agoraphobics in Motion (AIM) sponsors a network of support groups, principally in Michigan, but they're open to assisting the formation of new groups in any state.

1719 Crooks

Royal Oak, MI 48067

248-547-0400

www.aim-hq.org

My website, **www.anxietycoach.com**, is principally a source for self-help information, but has some listings of support groups, both on-line and face-to-face groups.

Additional resources to check include the following:

- local newspaper listings, i.e., the community calendar
- your physician
- your priest, minister, rabbi, etc.
- local departments of health and mental health
- community mental health centers
- Employee Assistance Programs at your job
- local chapters of the National Mental Health Association
- psychiatric departments of local hospitals
- the American Psychological Association
- the American Psychiatric Association
- state chapters of the two associations above

Once you've identified some groups in your community, take the time to visit each of them two or three times to see what they are like. Don't select (or reject) a group based on just one visit, because the meetings can vary considerably from week to week. If possible, call the contact person before you attend, introduce yourself, and get additional information.

Making advance contact with the group will probably make your first arrival there a little more comfortable, because you'll have already "met" one member, and you'll be a little better informed of what to expect.

Consider the following points when visiting a group.

- Does the group make new members and visitors feel welcome?
- Would I be comfortable sharing my struggles with these people? Can they help me? Can I help them?
- Are meetings held at a time and place reasonably convenient for me to attend?
- Is there helpful give-and-take in the group? Does the group give everyone a chance to participate without getting bogged down on just one or two individuals?
- Are people actually making progress as a result of their participation in the group?
- Do members set goals for themselves, and achieve them?
- Do group members refrain from offering each other advice about medications (leaving that to the prescribing physician) and instead focus on what they can do for themselves?
- Does the group provide current, reputable information about anxiety disorders from established sources?

....

About the Author

An expert in the treatment of anxiety disorders, **Dr. David Carbonell** has con-
ducted training and seminars for a wide variety of professional and consumer
groups throughout the United States. He is an avid proponent of self help for
people with anxiety problems and maintains a website (www.anxietycoach.com)
that offers extensive self-help materials for people with fears and phobias. Dr.
Carbonell, a clinical psychologist, is the founder and director of the Anxiety
Treatment Center, Ltd., which offers outpatient treatment for people suffering
from fears and phobias in Chicago. He is a member of the American
Psychological Association, the Anxiety Disorders Association of America, the
Association for Behavioral and Cognitive Therapies, and the International
Association for Cognitive Therapy.